AF580379

Man Ray's Paris Portraits: 1921-39

Man Ray's Paris Portraits: 1921-39

❖ ❖ ❖

Revised Edition

Timothy Baum

This publication is the catalog for the exhibition *Man Ray's Paris Portraits: 1921-39*, at the Salvador Dalí Museum in St. Petersburg, Florida, September 27th, 1997 to January 18th, 1998.

This exhibition is sponsored in part by NationsBank.

ISBN 0-9660353-0-5

Cover: *A Group of surrealists at Tzara's House*, 1930.

SALVADOR DALI MUSEUM EDITIONS

Cachet Man Ray

Cachet, as that which differentiates the specialty of one master's work or product from any and all of the others. In the early 1920s in Paris, one learned quickly that if you were to have your photographic portrait made, you would be wasting your time unless you gained yourself a sitting with the only resident master of this prestigious art: Man Ray. People flocked to him accordingly.

"Why Man Ray?", one can immediately inquire. Certainly because he was the finest of his profession. Finest, as in most proficient: measured by the highest quality of imagination mixed with technical prowess. With all such vigorous encomiums, one can still question how a foreigner, particularly one so recently arrived in Paris, could have such a resounding impact on a society so notorious for its obdurate rigidity and related judgmental barriers. And not only was this gentleman a foreigner, but a Dadaist as well. Imagine!

Man Ray, then. Fresh from New York, but seasoned to a certain level of European sophistication (and related fantasy) from such associations as his estranged Belgian-born wife, Adon Lacroix, and one grand friendship with the inimitable Marcel Duchamp. Thus did he arrive quite proudly on French soil in July of 1921, and never thereafter did he feel desirous of departing, except when the arrival of the German army in his beloved Paris tumbled all reality asunder.

By the end of 1921, Man had become an integral member of the Paris Dada group. He was the only American to fit snugly into its mischievous midst, and nimbly did he become one of its most enterprising participants. Within a few months of his arrival, a one-man show of his work was mounted at the Librairie Six gallery-bookshop, owned by a brother Dadaist, Philippe Soupault, and his wife, Mick. The exhibition evoked great enthusiasm within the Dada ranks, but not a single work was sold. Man Ray, a bit crestfallen but hardly defeated, took the advice of several friends and returned his attention to his ever-ready alternate career of studio photographer. Earlier he had taken (created!) the portraits of many of his Dada cronies. Also, he had photographed the work of various other artists such as Picabia and Jacques Villon to subsidize his quavering income. Quickly did news of his originality and adroitness with the camera spread. By the second year his breadth of subjects had expanded greatly. Represented (and proudly so!) were most of the superstars of the cultural community: James Joyce, Erik Satie, Juan Gris, Gertrude Stein, all of the Dadaists, Jean Cocteau, Léger, Matisse, Picasso—you name them! Painting was temporarily abandoned, but "rayographs" emerged to fulfill his imagination's extracurricular cravings, and soon the album *Les Champs Délicieux* had been produced in elegant fashion.

By the middle of 1922, *Vanity Fair* magazine had enlisted Man Ray as portraitist, and from June of that year until well into the following decade, his work appeared in its pages.

For the first several months, Man compromised with his spare budget, and performed his photographic activities in the confines of his hotel room. The bathroom and closet, furthermore, doubled up as his darkroom-laboratories. Nobody thought the worse of him. The wonderful, ceremonial group portrait of the Paris Dadaists in 1921 was posed in this very room, in fact, hideous wallpaper and all, and most of the aforementioned literary and art celebrities found little reason not to sit and relax there. Within a short time, however Man Ray was able to accelerate his ante, and moved to a charming duplex studio-apartment on the rue Campagne-Première.

This remained his base of operations for several years to come. Man Ray was finally home.

Again you might ask why Man Ray was awarded this instantaneous popularity. Immediately must I reiterate he was *that* proficient at the photographic calling. Prior to Man Ray's arrival, the main manner in which to have your personal portrait done was to don your best suit, or veil, lace collar, or brooch, and sit so solemnly in the chair at one of the vanity photographic studios. The two grandest were at Henri Martinies or *chez* Manuel Frères. Whichever you picked, the result would be much the same: a stiff-backed, overly-posed, somewhat agonizing experience. Usually the final print turned out somewhere between whimsical and downright funereal—rarely was either extreme the bewildered sitter's intention. A visit *chez* Man Ray was entirely another experience.

Man Ray, as I mused in an earlier text, did not take photographs, but created them. Each portrait was a separate little adventure; the resultant print of a work of art. No two sittings were alike for him, and every separate sitting was a form of intimate occasion. Neil Baldwin, in his biography, likens Man Ray to a hunter, his "mind set" that of "the sportsman out for a day in the field." I would further elaborate and state: Man Ray, as portrait photographer, was the consummate hunter, in love. By the end of the mid-1920s, few of the Parisian social and artistic hierarchy had not crossed the threshold of Man Ray's studio, to pose. If intimate photographic encounters could be created as love affairs, then Man Ray was the only Casanova (or Rasputin?) of photography since the nineteenth century's grand master, Nadar. Surely in the annals of achievement in twentieth century portraiture, Man Ray would have no equal.

Other photographers of the Parisian free-lance brigade would come and go with their respective, insular clienteles. The elegant Baron de Meyer was toasted in some circles; similarly, George Hoyningen-Huené. The only one who emerged to overlap occasionally with Man Ray's own immediate coterie was his ex-apprentice assistant, Berenice Abbott. Miss Abbott gained a definite popularity among the literary crowd in Paris. Her portraits were generally competent, even memorable from time to time, but rarely dynamic or lustrous. She tended to cease probing her subjects at the edges of their physical boundaries, and rarely penetrated to their psychological undercurrents. Man Ray, using their physical features as a point of departure, often exited just short of their hearts and souls.

As the years wore on, Man Ray continued with photography as his profession, but always with painting as at least an equal devotion. Often the two would shiveringly overlap, as in the results of many of his experimentation's with solarization. Meanwhile his boundaries as photographer continued to expand. Quickly his ingenuity was recognized and admired by the fashion houses and from early on he was working closely with such glamour designers as Poiret, Patou, le Long, and Man's personal friend, Elsa Schiaparelli. Similarly, throughout the two decades preceding the Second World War, his work was avidly sought by the fashion magazines: *Charm, Vogue, Harper's Bazaar*, etcetera, both in Europe and back in New York.

Throughout these same two decades Man became, and remained, the portrait-photographer-laureate of Paris (and, conceivably, the entire world). His reputation never retreated from the highest plateau, for not only did his technical skill remain consistently lofty, but his ever-imaginative approach to innovative poses and settings never waned, and always there was the excitement of being his next subject.

Man Ray's array of portrait subjects was as diverse as any single studio could ever dream to assemble. Though he was not a lavish socializer, more a lone wolf in fact, he managed to meet, mingle with, and usually delight a cross-section of people from every stratum of society, and every corner of the arts. Where his earliest portfolio of subjects was mostly limited to writers and painters, it soon spread to the neighboring constellations of architects, musicians, and composers (Satie, Stravinsky, Antheil, Milhaud, Tailleferre, Georges Auric; indelibly the wonderful double-portrait of Clément Doucet and Jean Wiéner, elegantly posed with their miniature practice pianos); and actors and dancers and nightclub performers (Barbette, for example, and always the ebullient Kiki de Montparnasse, perhaps his most favorite subject of all!).

Greatness of reputation is always the surest disperser of austere social barricades in the grander circles of Paris society. From the early years onward, Man was accepted by one aristocratic celebrity or family after another. First came the eccentric but captivating Marquise Casati, then the supremely elegant Comte Etienne de Beaumont who befriended our hero and invited him to photographically immortalize his gala parties and balls. Similarly did Man visit the homes of the Comtesse Greffuhle (once considered the most beautiful woman in France by Marcel Proust, who used her as role model for at least two of the more scintillating Guermantes ladies in his epic novel, now on in years, but still youthful and inquisitive enough to entreat Man Ray to teach her how to develop photographs in her personal, makeshift darkroom: a noble adventure indeed!). Also the Comte and Comtesse Pecci-Blunt, the Comtesse de Chévigné and her entourage, the recently widowed Duchesse de Gramont, and eventually the great patrons of the arts, the charming, convivial Vicomte and Vicomtesse (Charles and Marie-Laure) de Noailles, who remained ever-loyal and encouraging friends.

As the 1920s ended joltingly with the crash of the world's economic markets, an immediate sobriety cast its pall upon the frivolities of the wild and carefree era, and many suffered accordingly. Luckily for Man Ray, as premier portrait photographer of the land, vanity still prevailed to outduel the dwindled pocketbook, and still the parade of clients wended on. Surrealism had superseded Dada, and new faces appeared each successive season: Dalí and Miró; de Chirico (now pioneer) and Tanguy; Meret Oppenheim, René Crevel, Magritte, René Char, Victor Brauner, the *ingenue* Gisèle Prassinos: an entire roll-call.

Generally, as the new generation of talent emerged from their cocoons, Man Ray was always there with his camera to catch them in their glories: Huxley, T. S. Eliot, Virginia Woolf and other Londoners passing through town for a visit; visiting grand masters as Kurt Schwitters and Kandinsky; a never-aging Picasso, and graying but ever-twinkling Picabia. Hardly did the rustiness of the Depression years greatly tarnish the sparkle of the personality parade that always made Paris the pinnacle city of high style and excitement.

Rarely did Man Ray stray from his limitless domains of preferred subject matters: artists and writers, glamorous people of society. One interesting exception—simply because Man Ray was a particularly non-political world citizen—was the series of portraits he made of the Socialist Prime Minister of France, Monsieur Léon Blum, but Blum was a close, personal friend with whom Man spent parts of his summer vacations.

In his autobiography (*Self Portrait*), Man Ray suggests that he strongly differentiated between those who he charged for his photographic services as a matter of course (his usual studio clients), and those who he photographed for the sheer pleasure of their company: most personal friends and confederates, as well as anybody he truly admired. The exceptions were the few of the latter category who were either exceptionally well-heeled, or the occasional person whose career Man felt had previously advanced as a result of earlier photographic assistance on his behalf (Gertrude Stein was an example of this minute category, and evidently was not at all pleased with the distinction).

Sometimes Man Ray's portraits coincided with the greater moments of his subjects' careers or lives (James Joyce at the time of the publication of *Ulysses*, Sinclair Lewis subsequent to winning the Pulitzer Prize for Literature, The Duchess of Windsor soon after her historic marriage, etcetera). Once did Man have the opportunity to immortalize the grandeur of an important personage at the time of his death: the stately 1922 deathbed portrait of Marcel Proust. Again, it was certainly a tribute to Man Ray's reputation that in this earliest period of his residency in Paris he was chosen for this honor (hardly was Proust's inner sanctum bedroom the romping ground for a visiting American Dadaist!).

Throughout his career as portrait photographer, there was always an endless dribble of schemes and suggestions by others concerning how Man could enhance his career and related earnings. Except for the inevitable acceptance of contracts with fashion houses and fashion magazines, he politely excused himself from such offers. One of the more diverting proposals was that proffered by Aleister Crowley (once described to Hemingway as "the wickedest man in the world"). Man Ray's bemused description of the incident in his autobiography is worth the re-telling as follows:

"There was a strange character, Aleister Crowley, whom I'd heard of in connection with various suspect activities in London and New York. We were sitting in a café with some friends; he took me aside to speak more confidentially. He knew many wealthy women who came to him for horoscopes. We could work together, he said—why not tell those that wished to be photographed that I required their horoscope in order to portray them properly; on his side he would tell a prospective client for a horoscope that he needed a portrait of her to complete his analysis. As I did not need the extra business, the proposition was not adopted." Suffice it to say that, blessedly, Man Ray did not need to resort to gimmickry to assert the novelty of the grandeur of his talent.

As a final note, I must make brief mention of the self-portraits of Man Ray. Unlike many other photographers, Man Ray's studies of himself created a miniature, abridged autobiography of his entire adult life. The early (1924), rather formal self-study shows us a well-dressed man approaching thirty-five years of age who was caught in the void between early success and related lingering doubts as to the course of his future destiny. Later self-portraits, not so analytic, show us Man Ray in his changing milieux: in the surrealists' midst, at the grand balls, relaxing in cafés, proud in his studios, etcetera. The final study presented here depicts a sober and dignified Paul Eluard, one of Man Ray's most cherished Paris friends and loyal supporters, back in military attire after twenty civilian years of merry and meritous poetic activity and achievement, resigned to go to war again.

Thus was one of the most beautiful and purposeful liaisons of the present century: Man Ray's two decades of mutual love and admiration, between the two wars, with and within the dreams and realities of the Ville de Paris. Unlike most such romantic tales, we have a vivid visual record of all of its characters and great moments: Man Ray's Paris portraits, hopefully brought back to life for you within these pages once again.

Timothy Baum

1. *Philippe Soupault*, 1921. Pioneer Dada poet and editor; co-owner of the bookshop/gallery, Librairie Six, where Man Ray had his first Paris one-man exhibition in December 1921, the same year as his arrival from America.

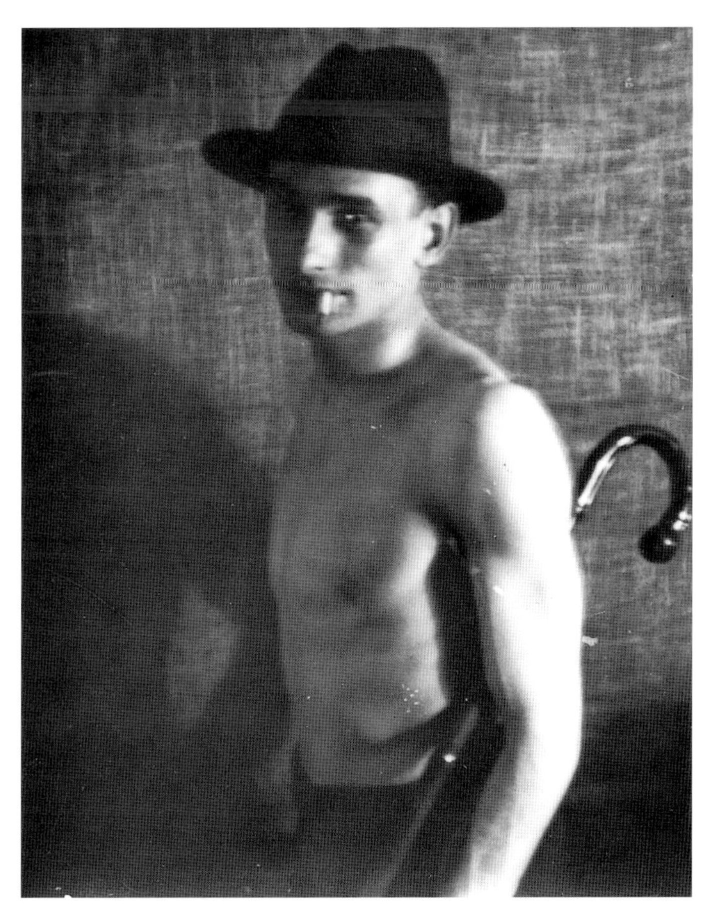

2. *A Group of Paris Dadaists*, 1921. Fun-loving, but always interesting and intelligent as well, the zany, elegant Paris Dada brigade! Seated, from left to right: Paul Eluard, Jacques Rigaut, "Mick" Soupault, Georges Ribemont-Dessaignes; standing: Paul Chadourne, Tristan Tzara, Philippe Soupault and Serge Charchoune.

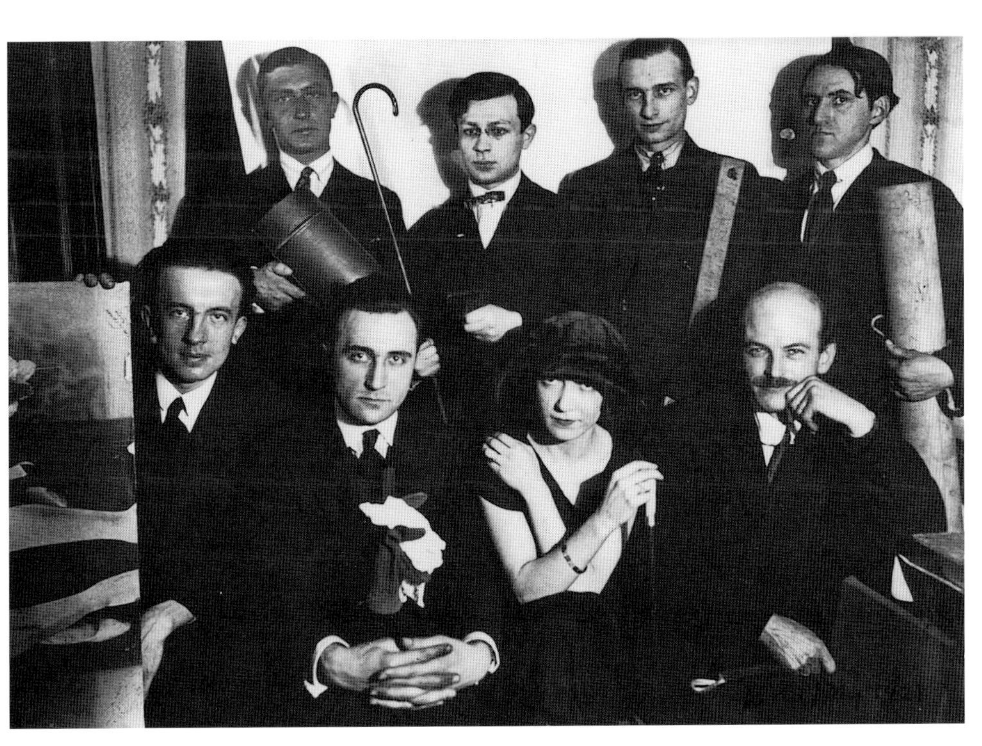

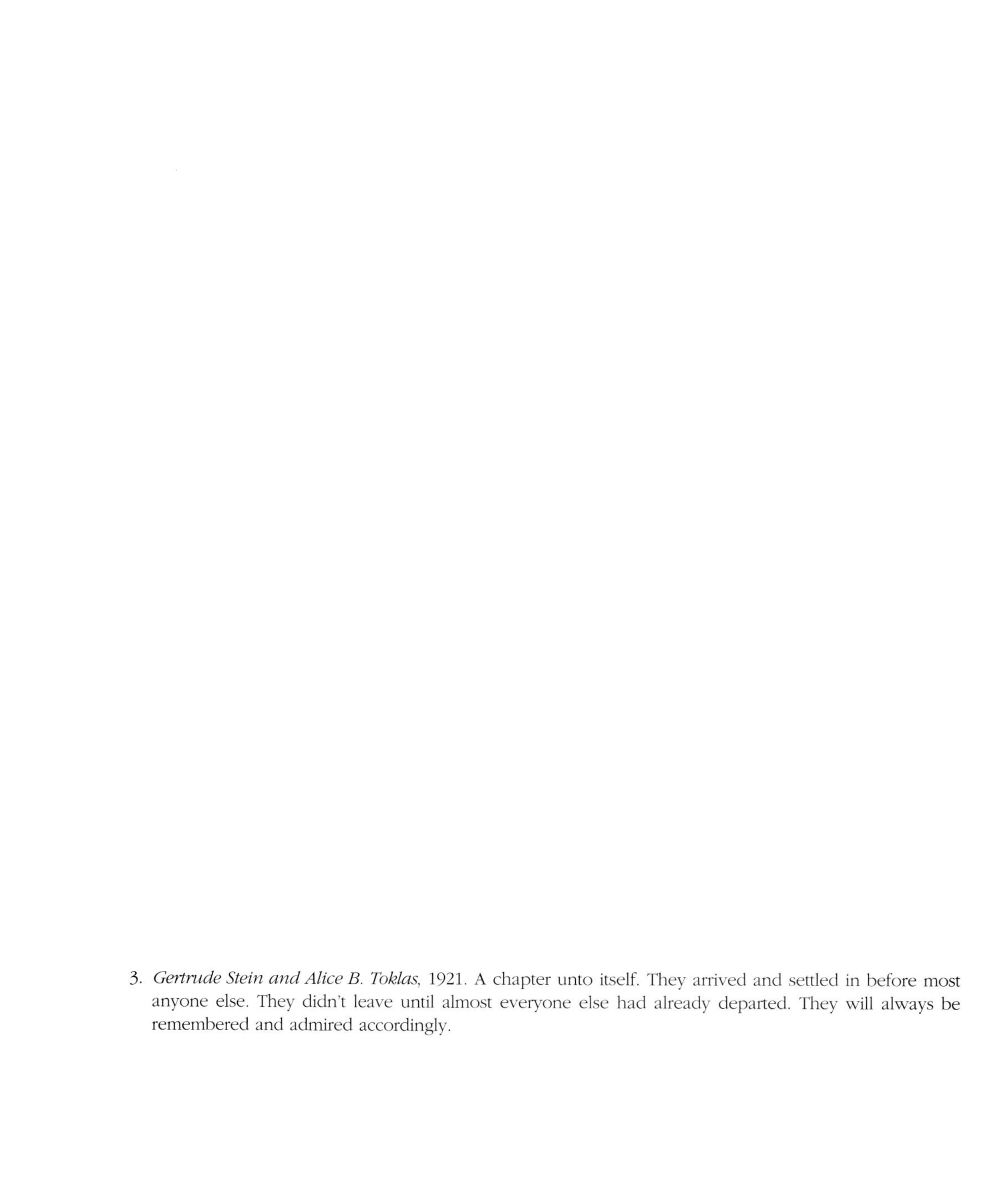

3. *Gertrude Stein and Alice B. Toklas*, 1921. A chapter unto itself. They arrived and settled in before most anyone else. They didn't leave until almost everyone else had already departed. They will always be remembered and admired accordingly.

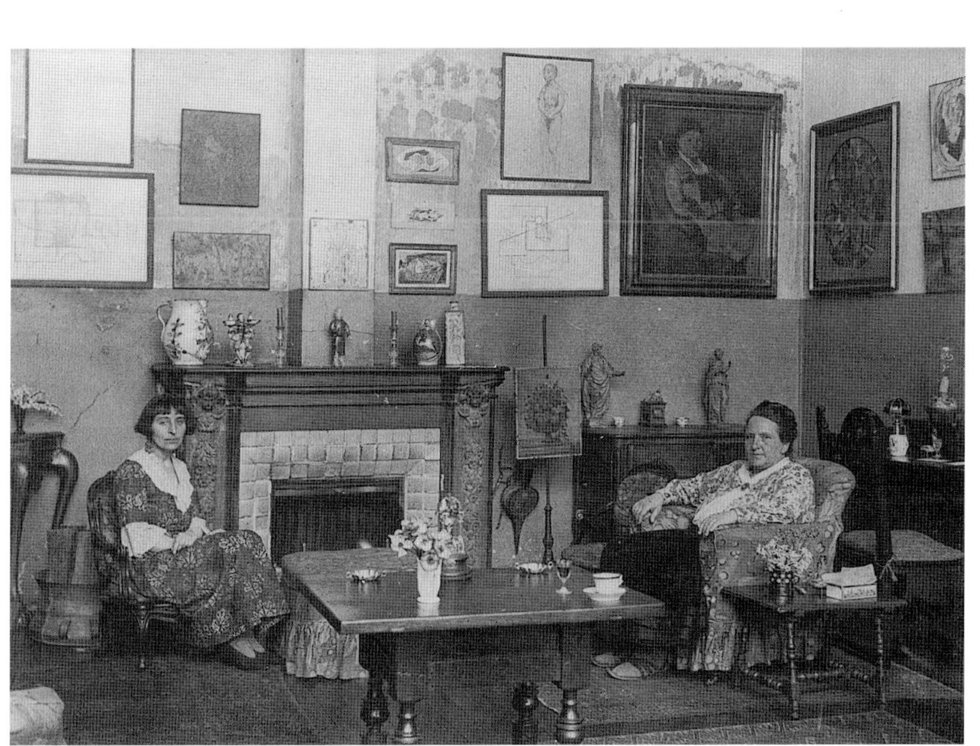

4. *Georges Braque*, 1922. Man Ray met and photographed them all (well, almost). Braque, proud and erect and strong, continuing his work amidst the uncertainty of all the newer tendencies and movements tumbled upon the madcap, postwar Paris scene, undaunted.

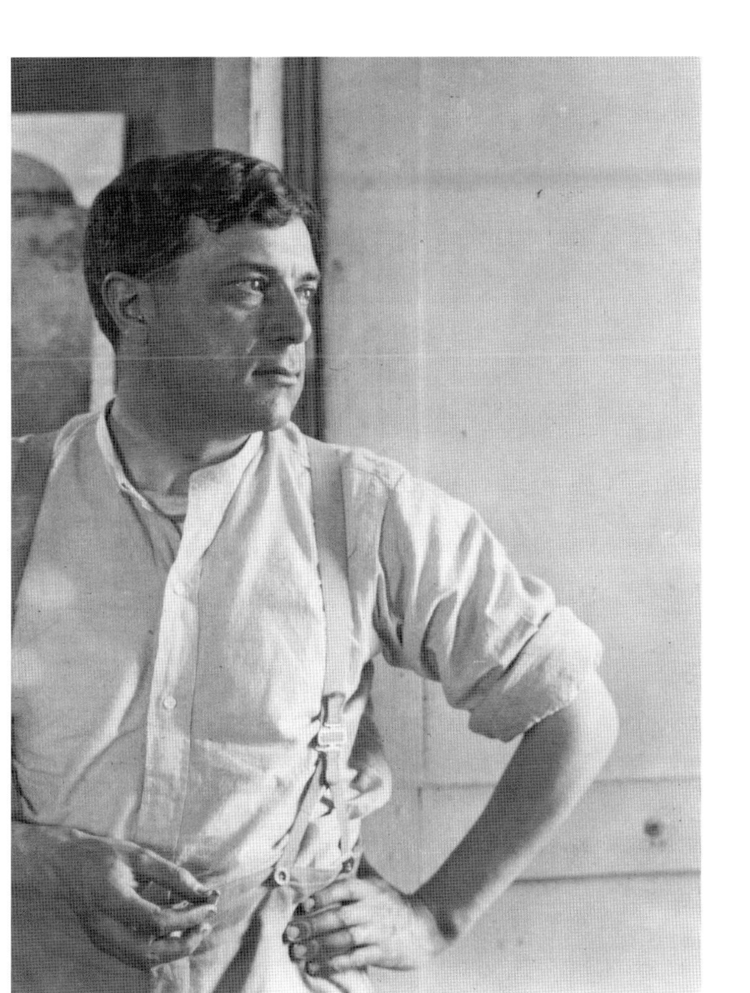

5. *Pierre Mac Orlan*, 1922. Novelist and man of letters, member of the ever-carefree Montparnasse café set.

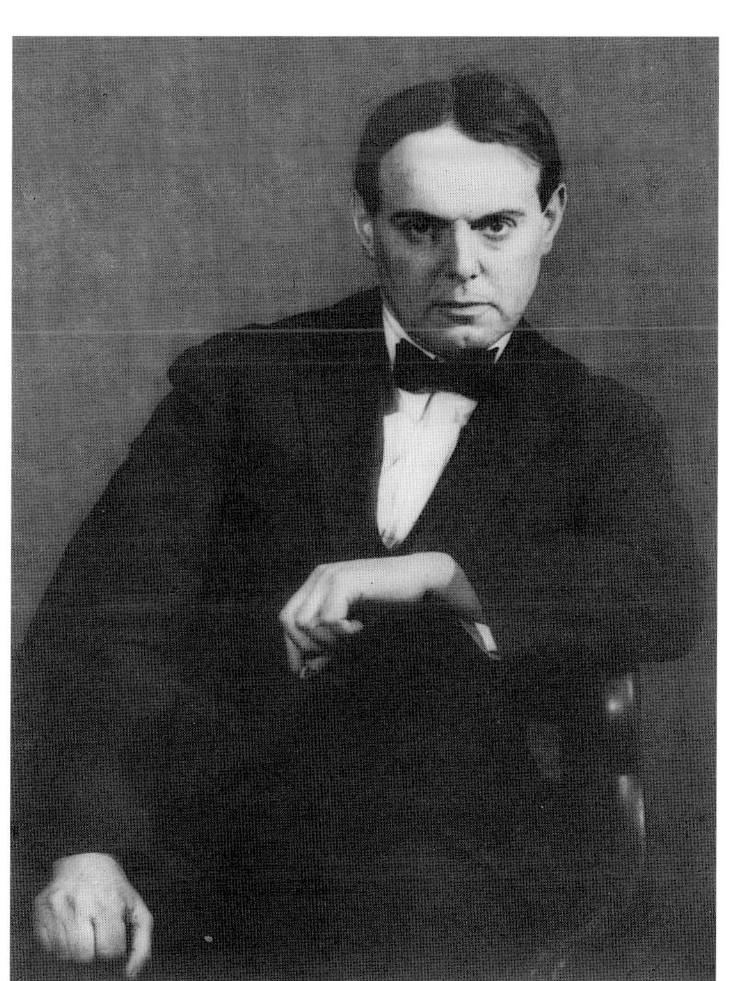

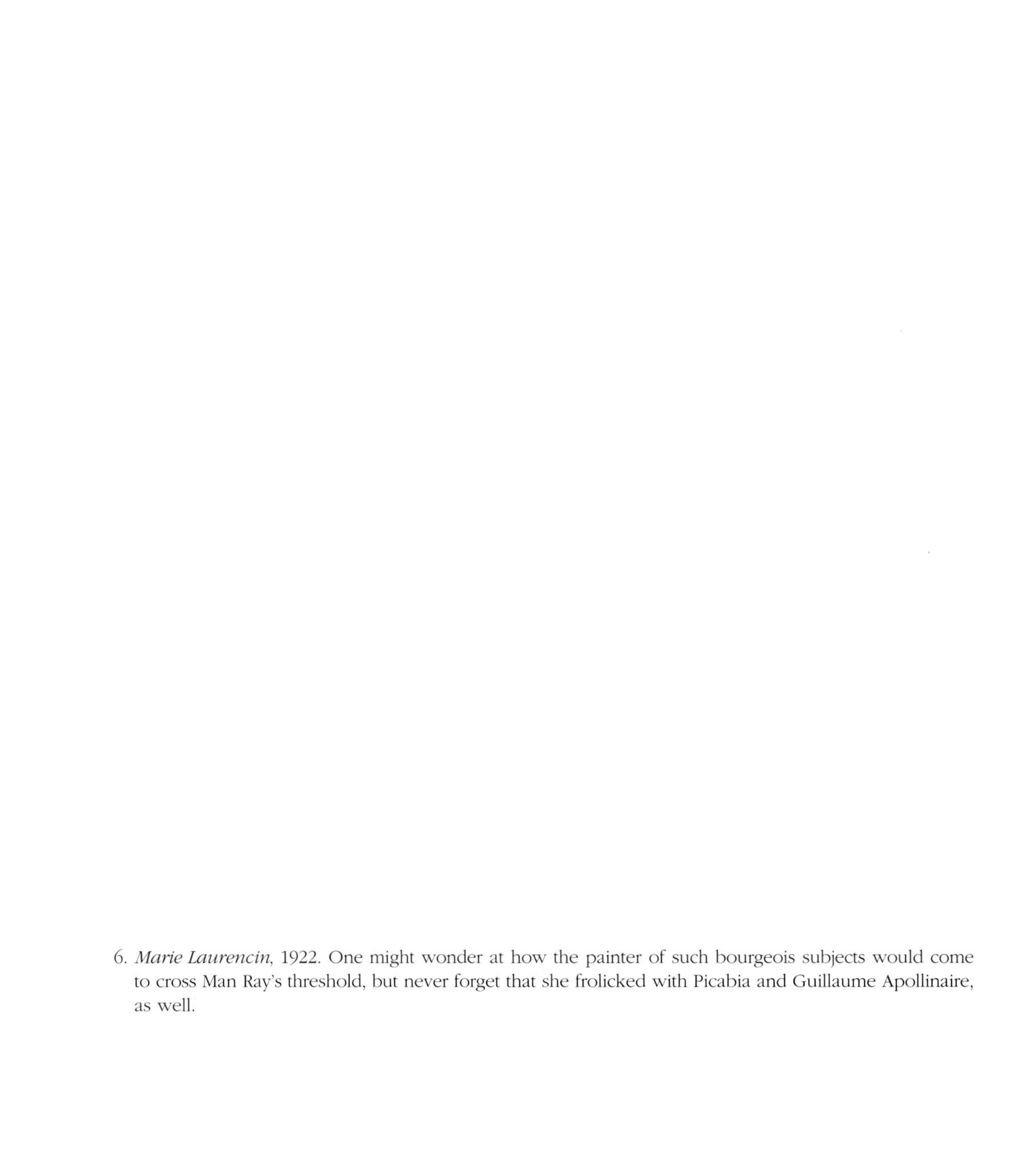

6. *Marie Laurencin*, 1922. One might wonder at how the painter of such bourgeois subjects would come to cross Man Ray's threshold, but never forget that she frolicked with Picabia and Guillaume Apollinaire, as well.

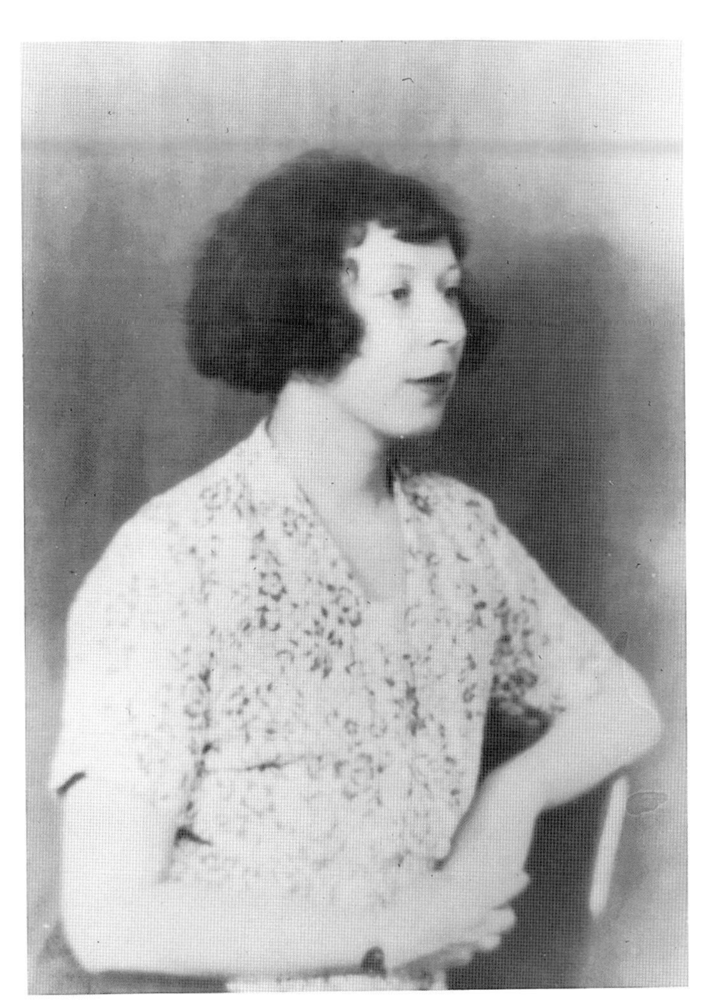

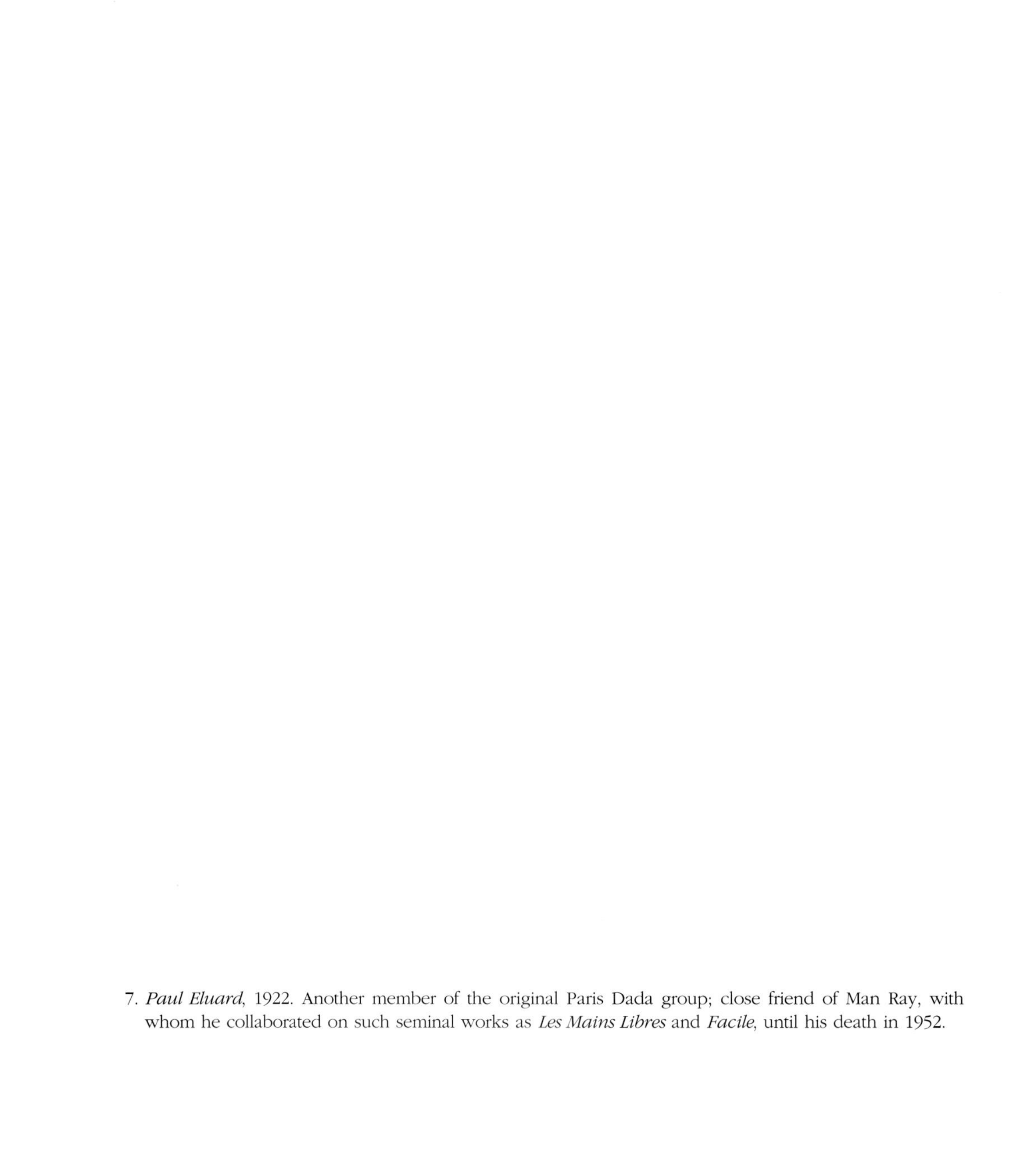

7. *Paul Eluard*, 1922. Another member of the original Paris Dada group; close friend of Man Ray, with whom he collaborated on such seminal works as *Les Mains Libres* and *Facile*, until his death in 1952.

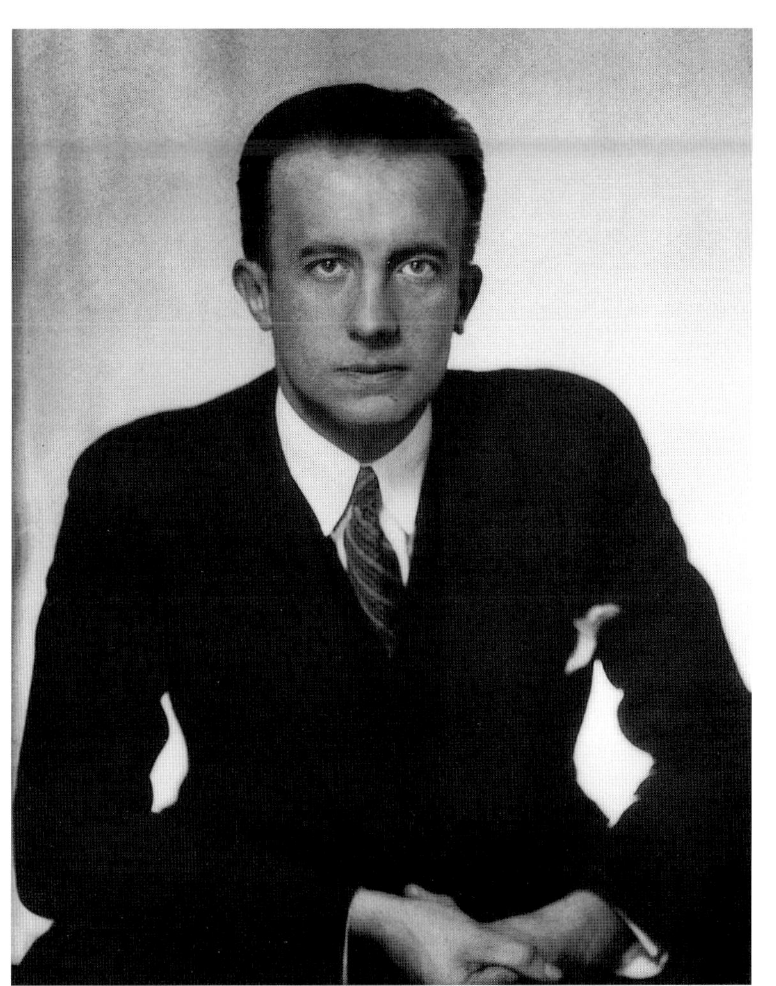

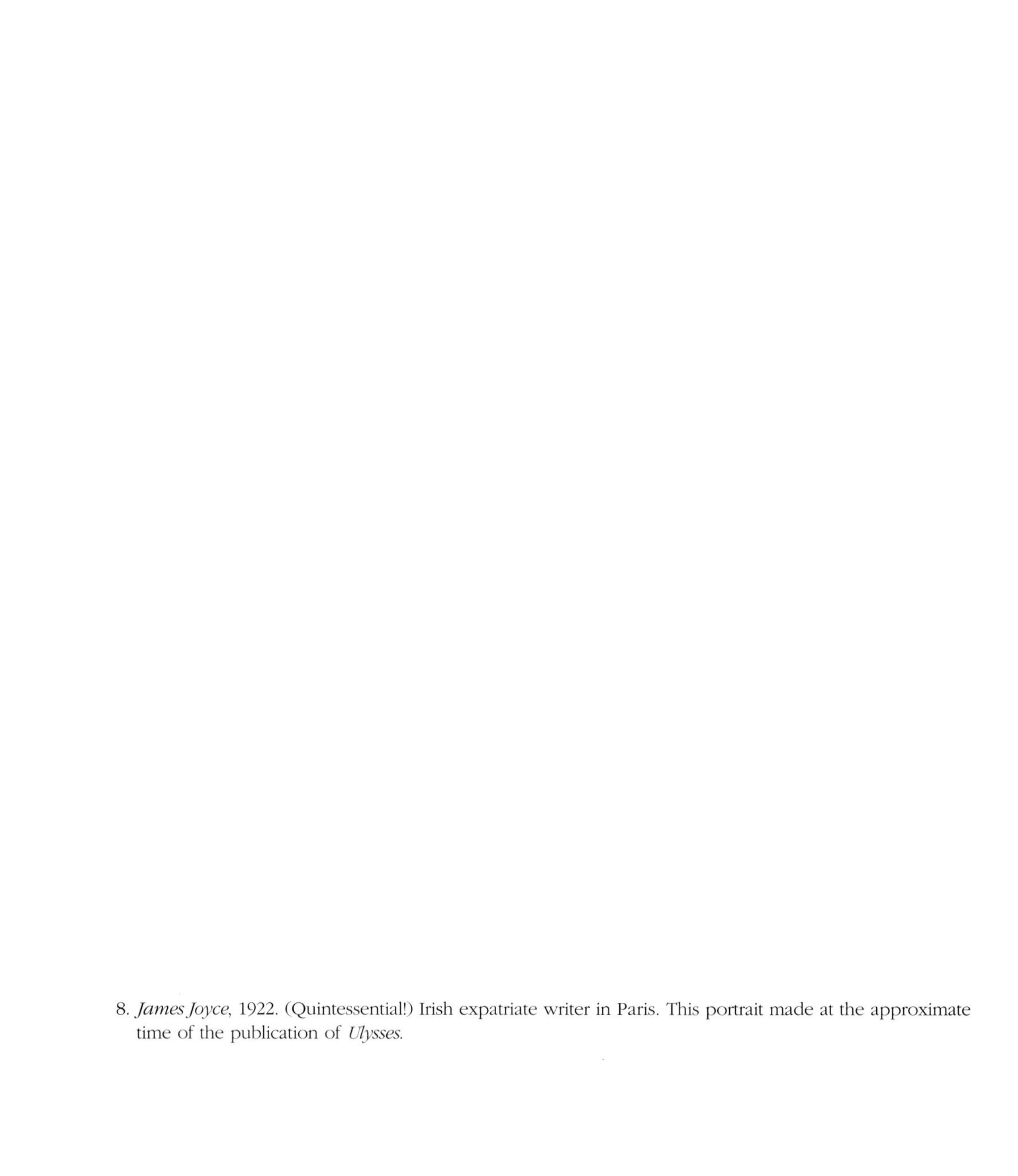

8. *James Joyce*, 1922. (Quintessential!) Irish expatriate writer in Paris. This portrait made at the approximate time of the publication of *Ulysses.*

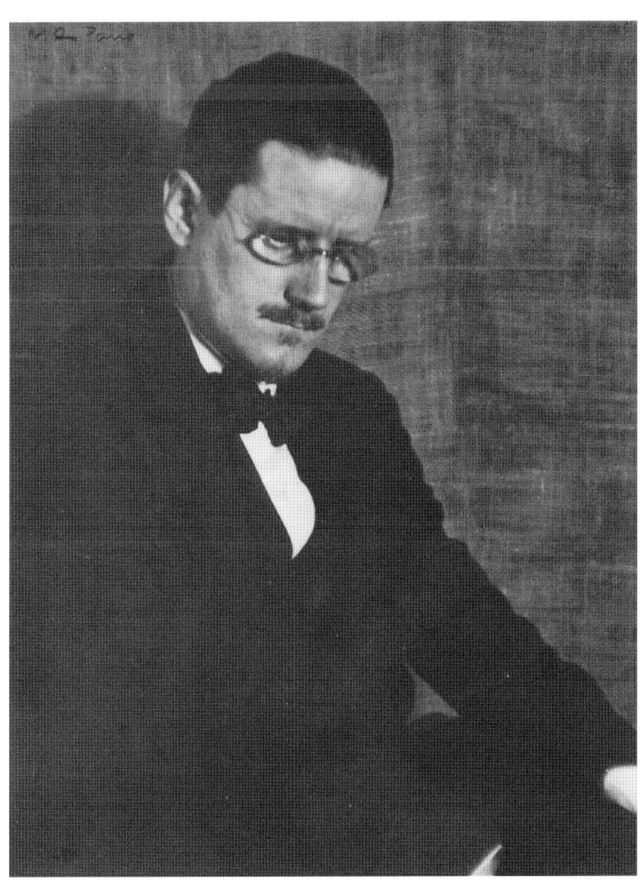

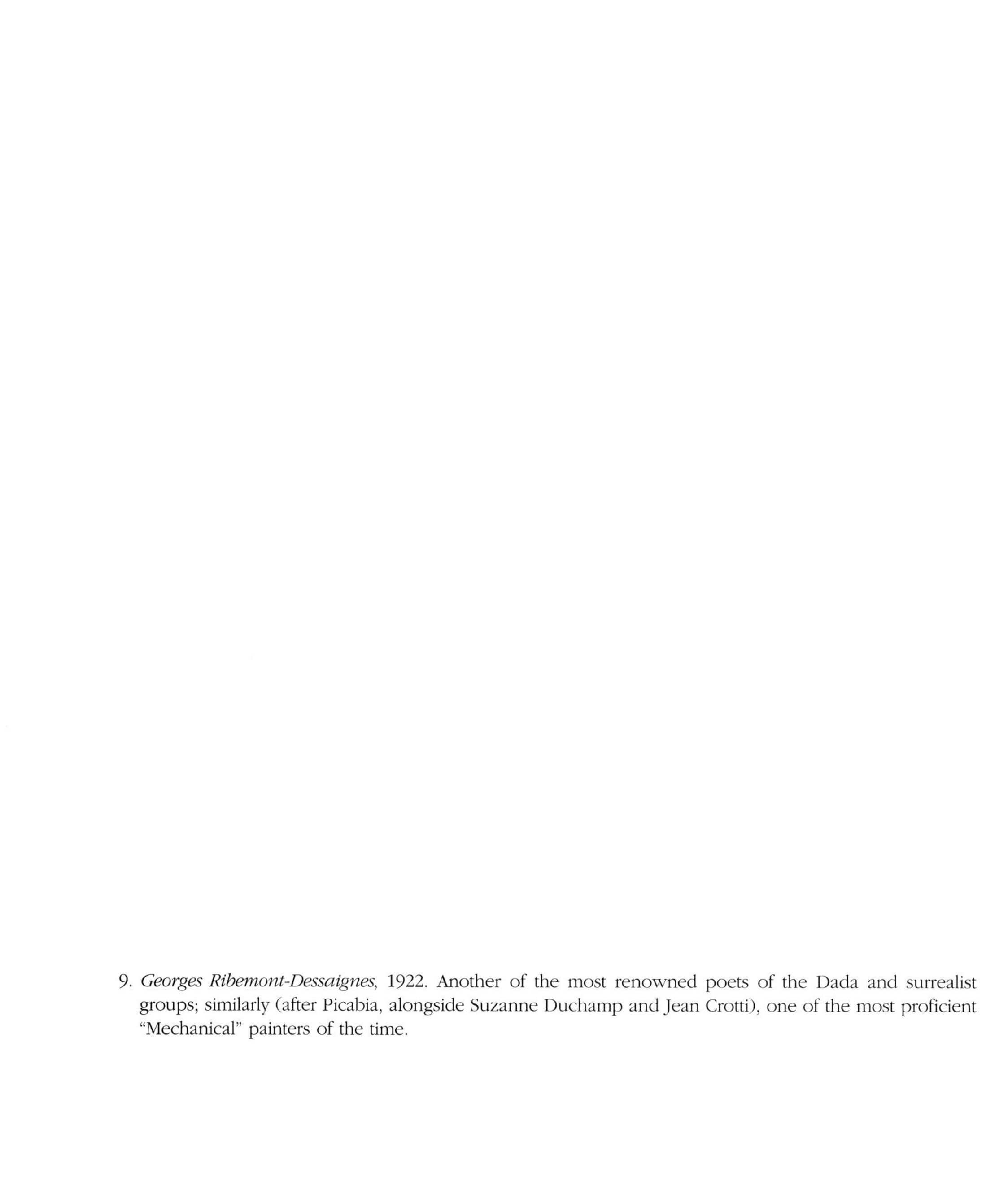

9. *Georges Ribemont-Dessaignes*, 1922. Another of the most renowned poets of the Dada and surrealist groups; similarly (after Picabia, alongside Suzanne Duchamp and Jean Crotti), one of the most proficient "Mechanical" painters of the time.

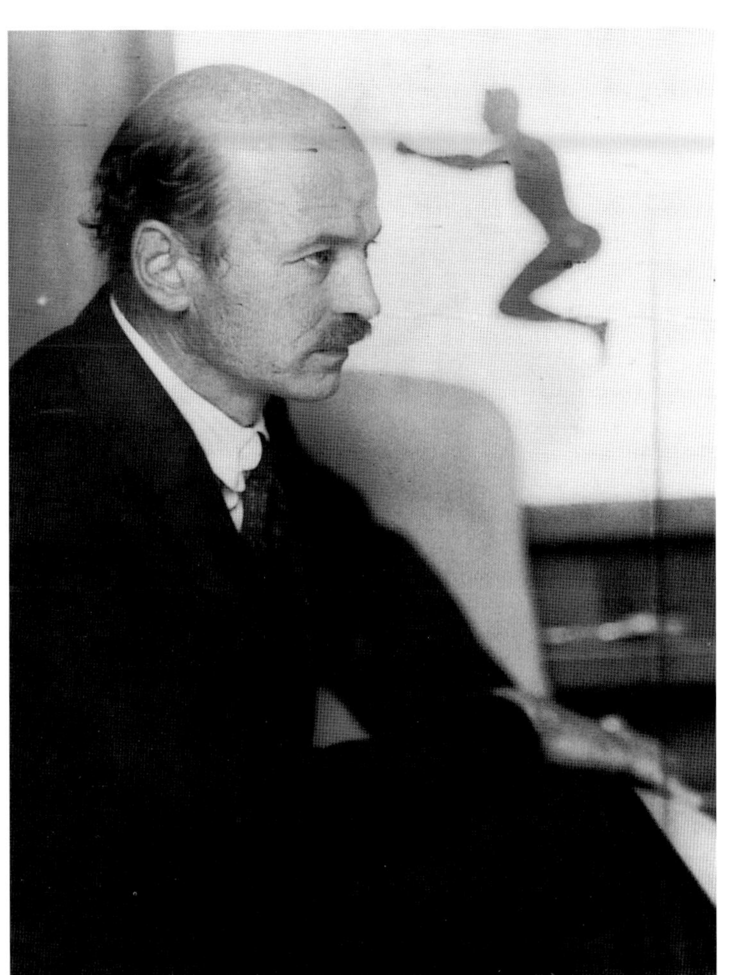

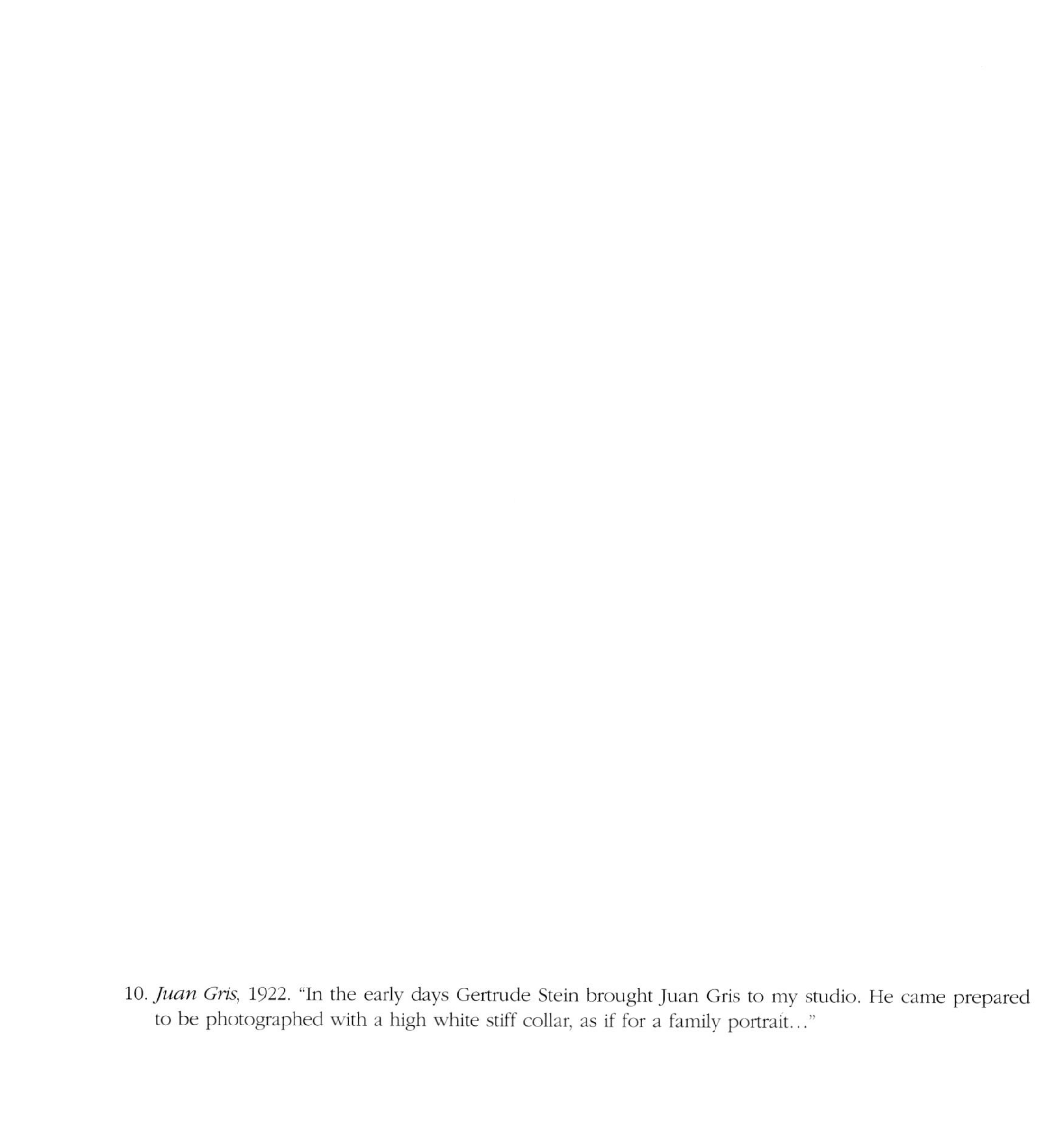

10. *Juan Gris*, 1922. "In the early days Gertrude Stein brought Juan Gris to my studio. He came prepared to be photographed with a high white stiff collar, as if for a family portrait..."

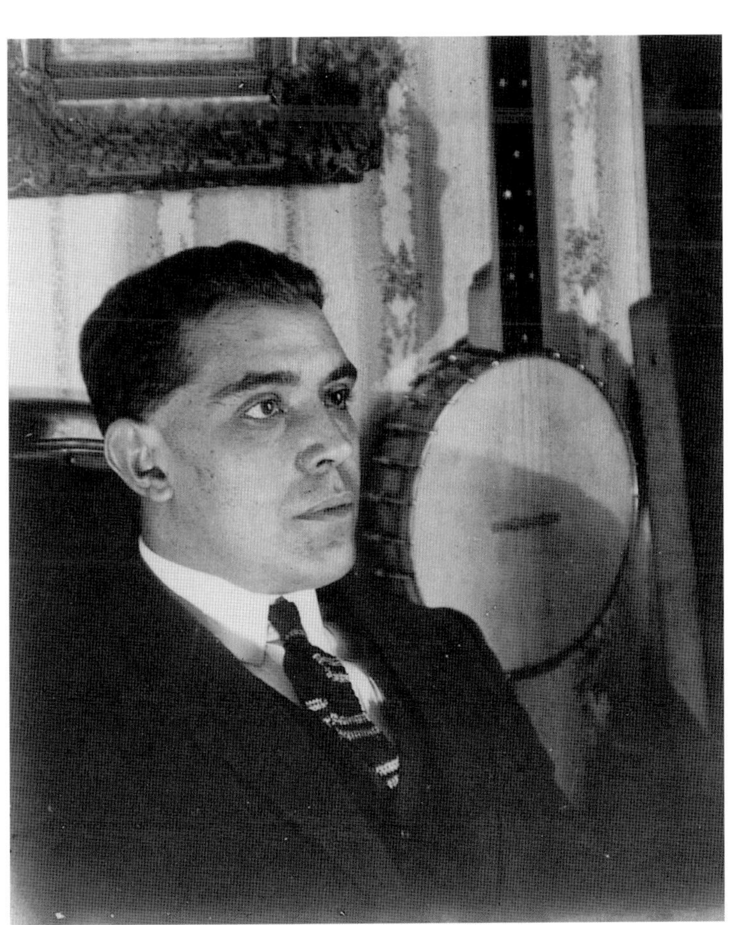

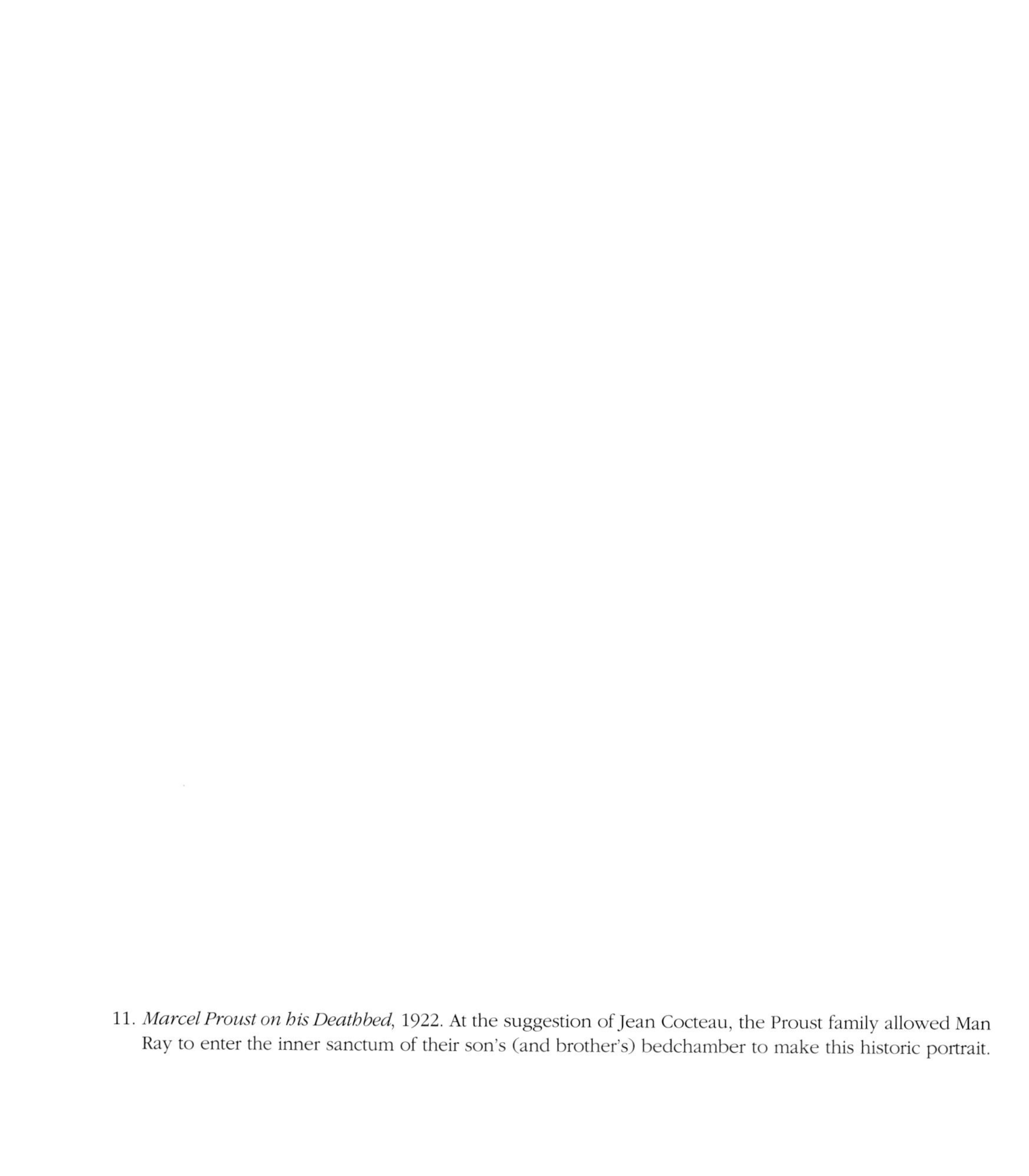

11. *Marcel Proust on his Deathbed*, 1922. At the suggestion of Jean Cocteau, the Proust family allowed Man Ray to enter the inner sanctum of their son's (and brother's) bedchamber to make this historic portrait.

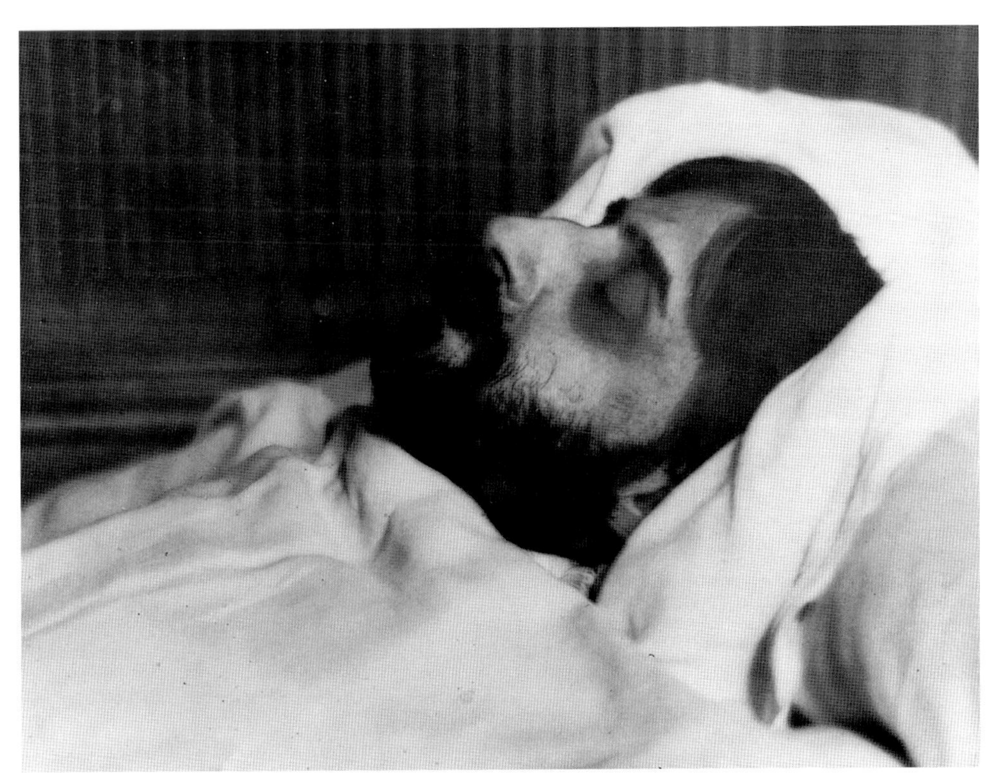

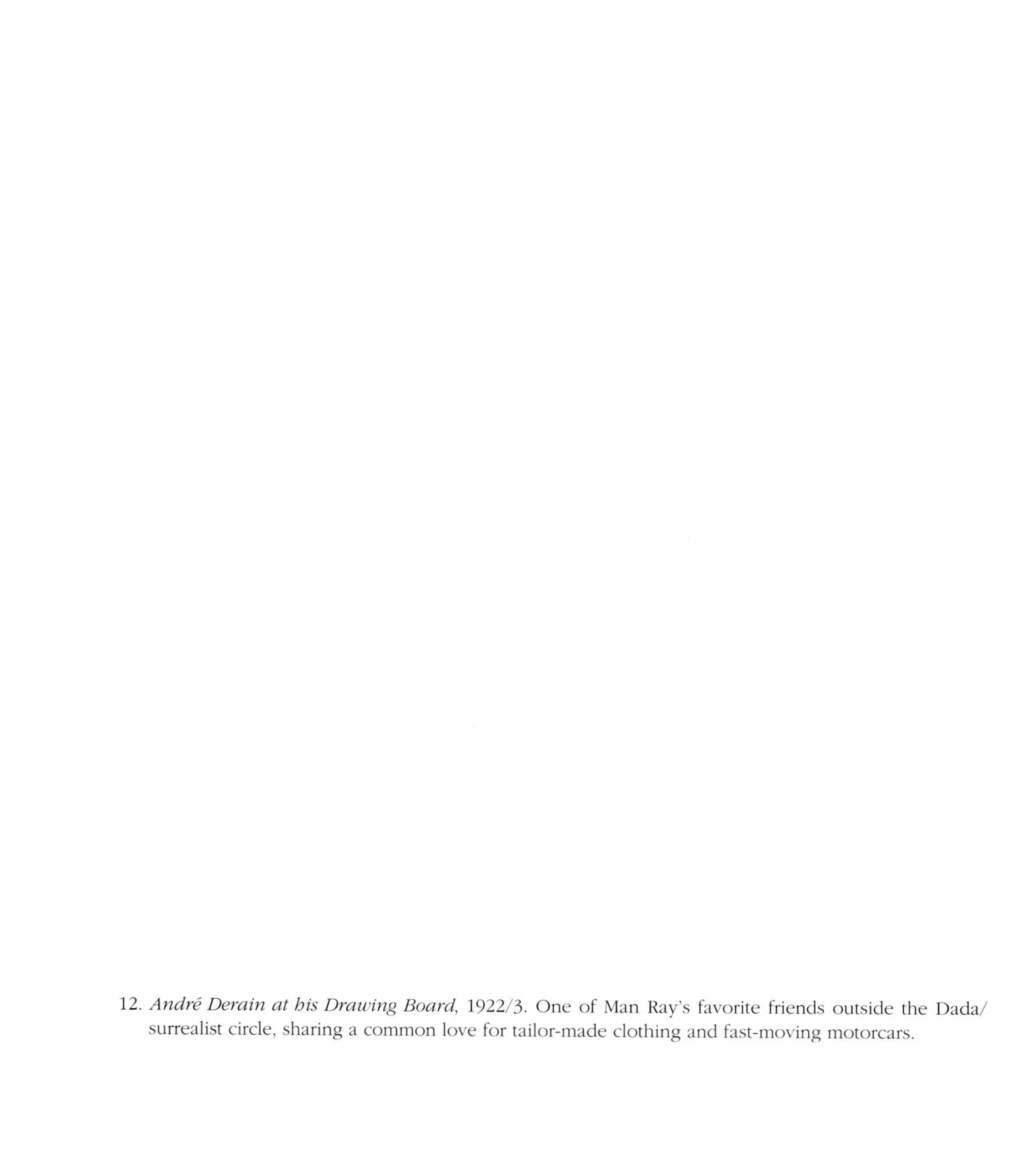

12. *André Derain at his Drawing Board,* 1922/3. One of Man Ray's favorite friends outside the Dada/surrealist circle, sharing a common love for tailor-made clothing and fast-moving motorcars.

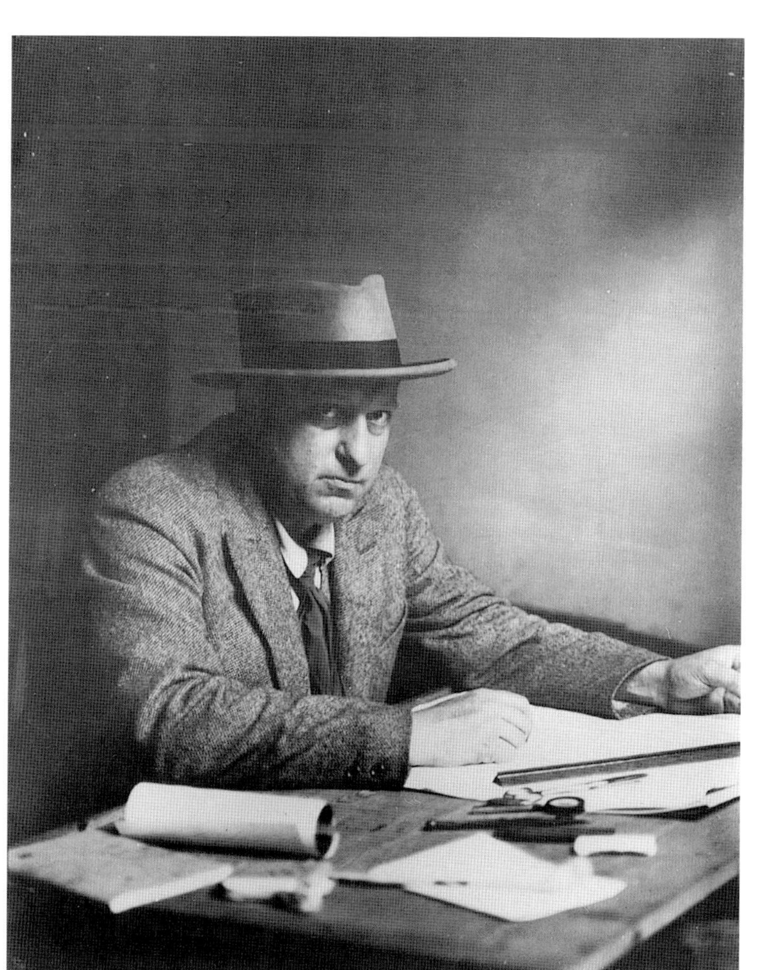

13. *Jacques Rigaut,* c. 1923. Ah yes, the charming and debonair Jacques Rigaut. Elegant, witty, personable, capricious: he died by his own hand soon after the Stock Market crash in 1929, the glamour of his café-society world choked to a halt, and he in mourning.

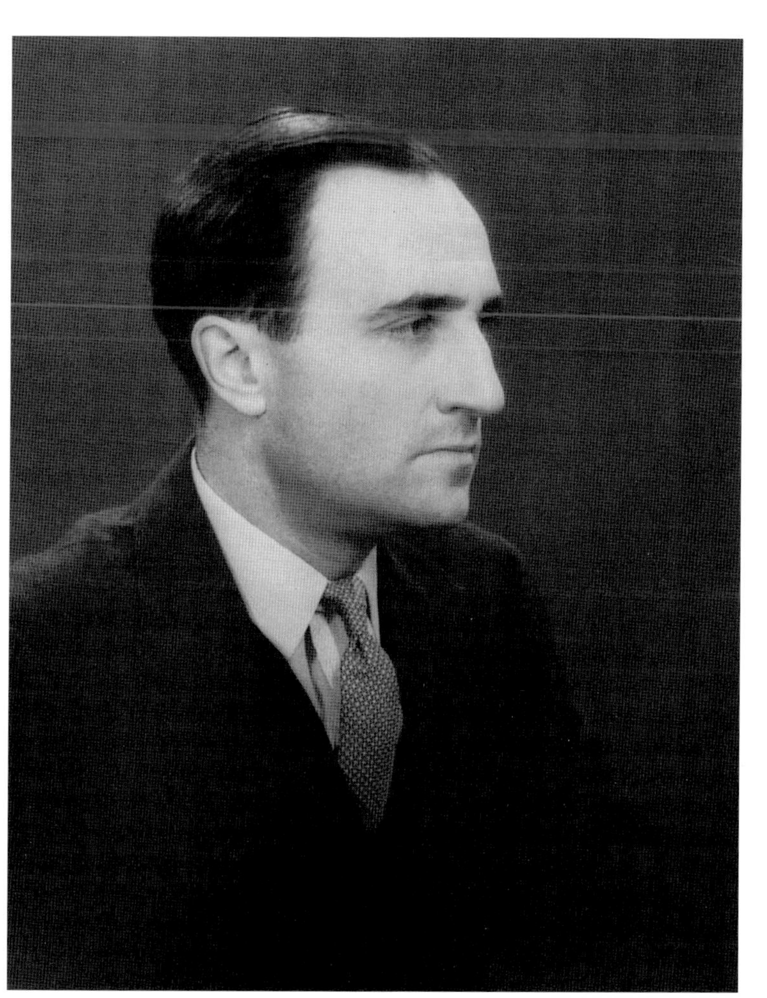

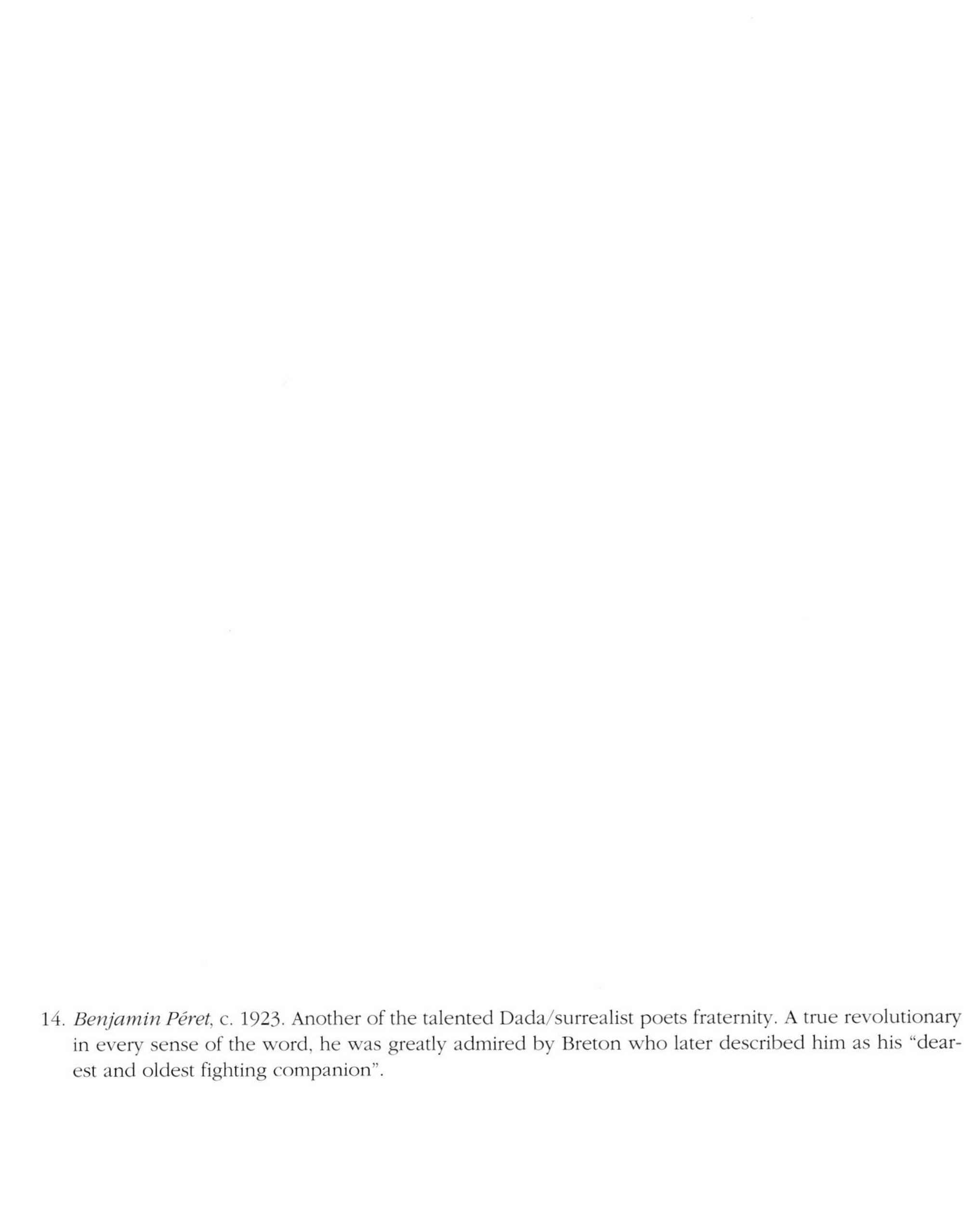

14. *Benjamin Péret*, c. 1923. Another of the talented Dada/surrealist poets fraternity. A true revolutionary in every sense of the word, he was greatly admired by Breton who later described him as his "dearest and oldest fighting companion".

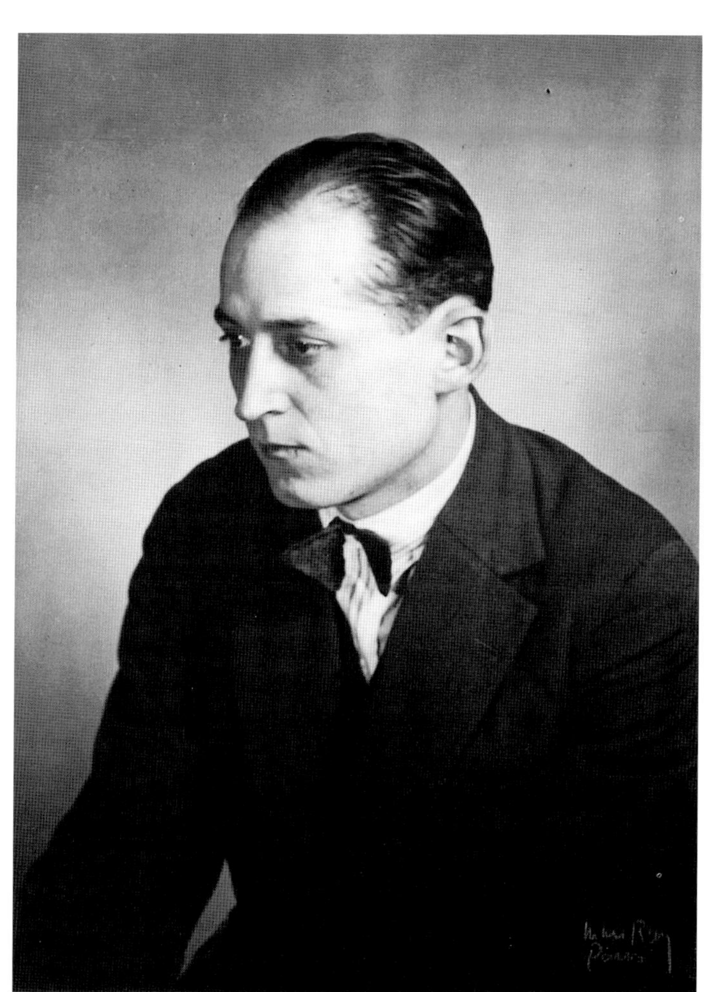
Man Ray
Paris

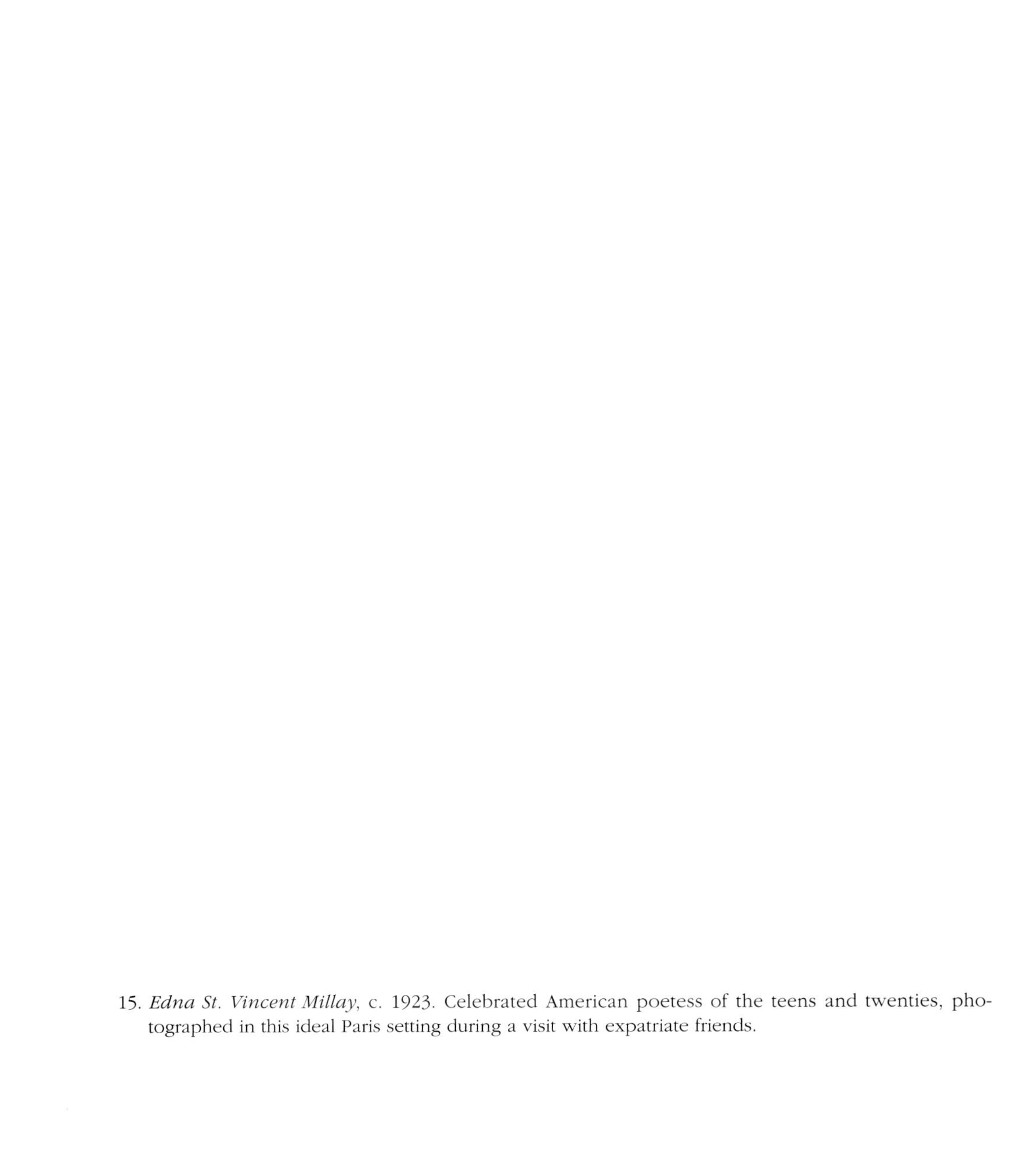

15. *Edna St. Vincent Millay*, c. 1923. Celebrated American poetess of the teens and twenties, photographed in this ideal Paris setting during a visit with expatriate friends.

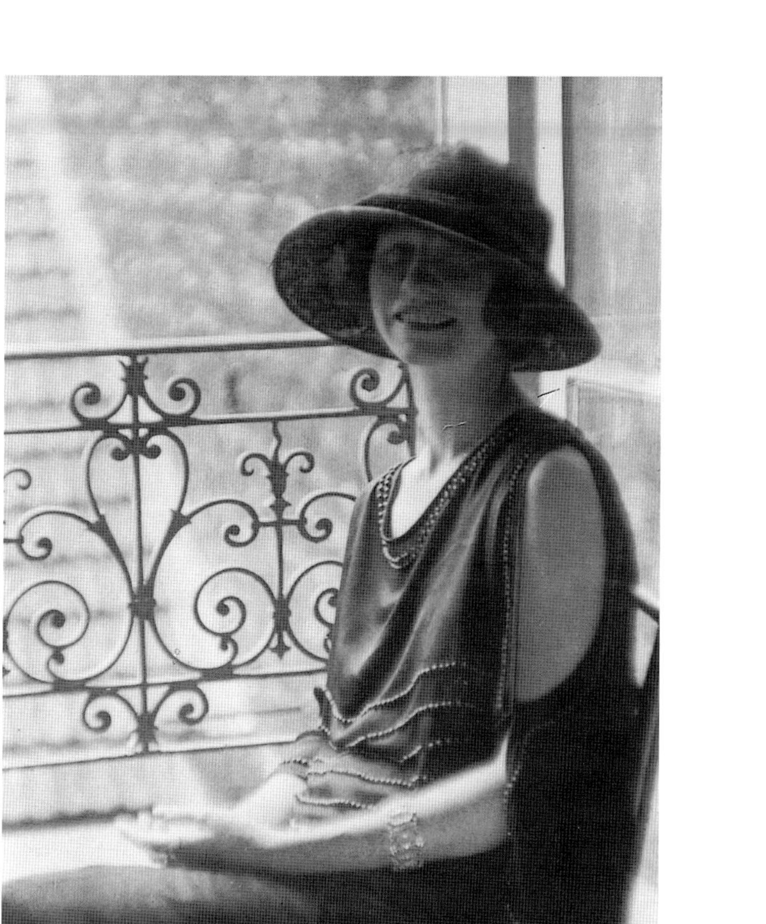

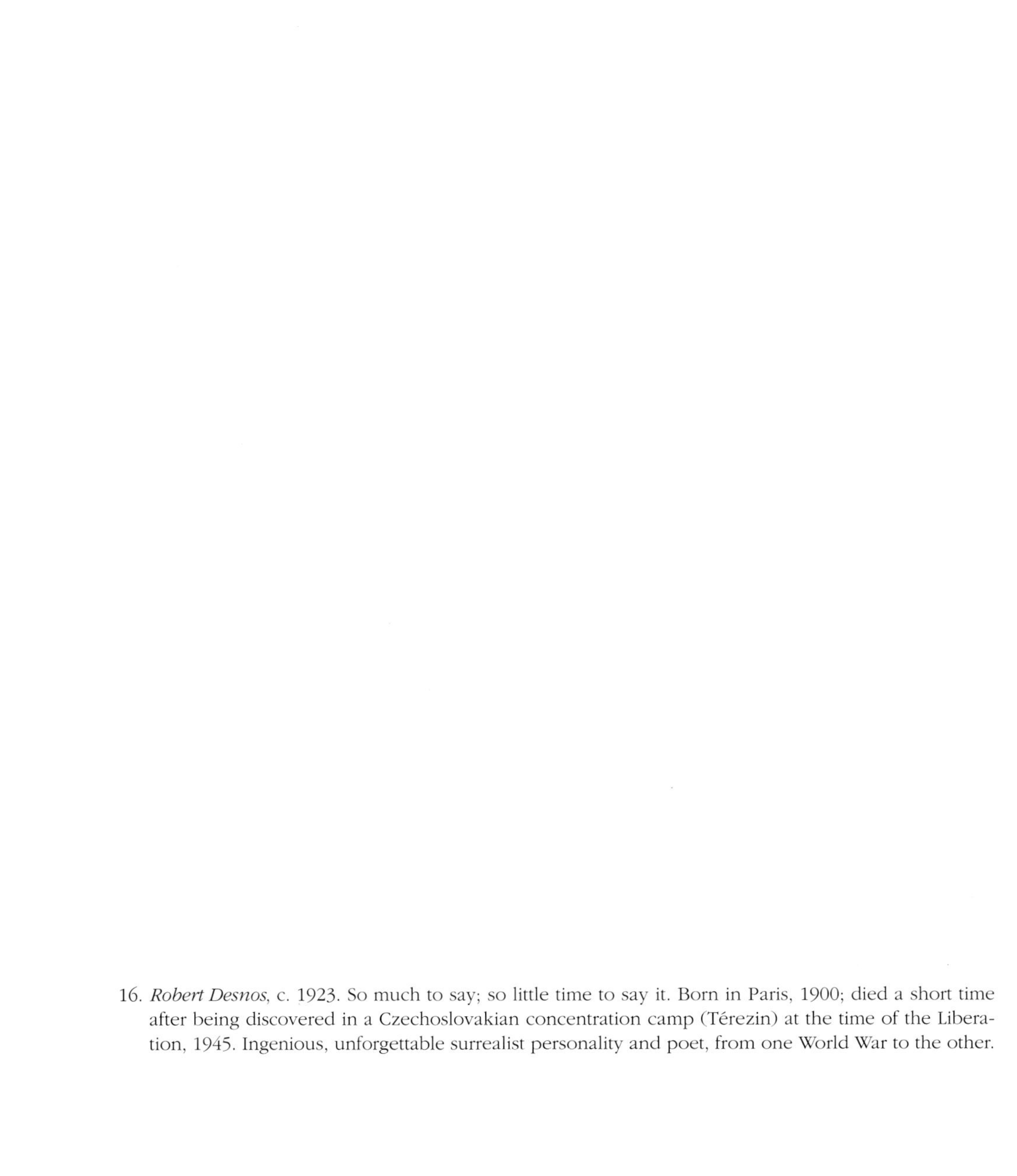

16. *Robert Desnos*, c. 1923. So much to say; so little time to say it. Born in Paris, 1900; died a short time after being discovered in a Czechoslovakian concentration camp (Térezin) at the time of the Liberation, 1945. Ingenious, unforgettable surrealist personality and poet, from one World War to the other.

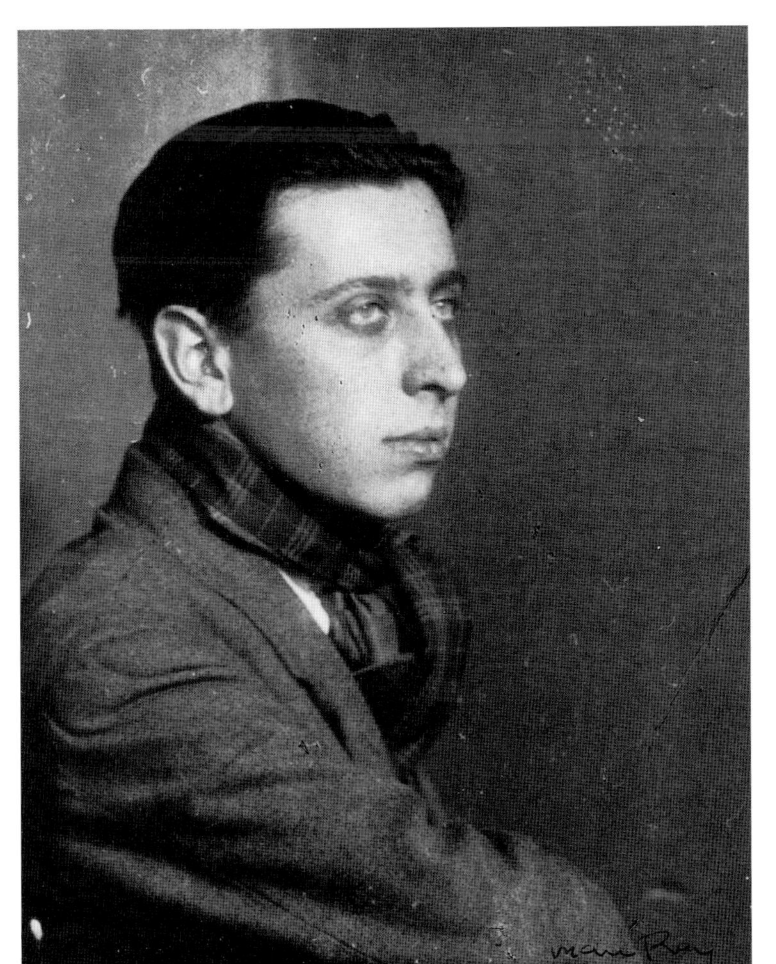
man Ray

17. *Margaret Anderson and Jane Heap*, 1923/4. Coeditors of *The Little Review*, one of the most influential "little magazines" of the 1920s. Founded by Anderson in Chicago in 1914, the magazine subsequently moved to New York, and then in 1923 to Paris. Between 1918 and 1920 *The Little Review* published Joyce's *Ulysses* in twenty-three installments, three issues of which were confiscated by the U.S postal authorities: "Like a burning at the stake," according to Miss Anderson.

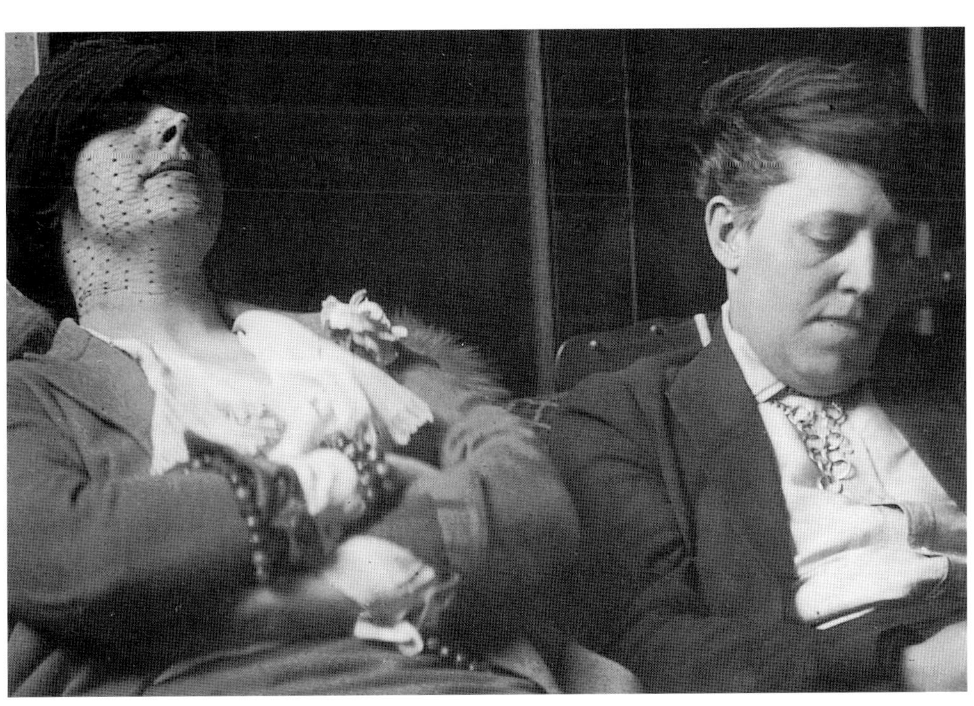

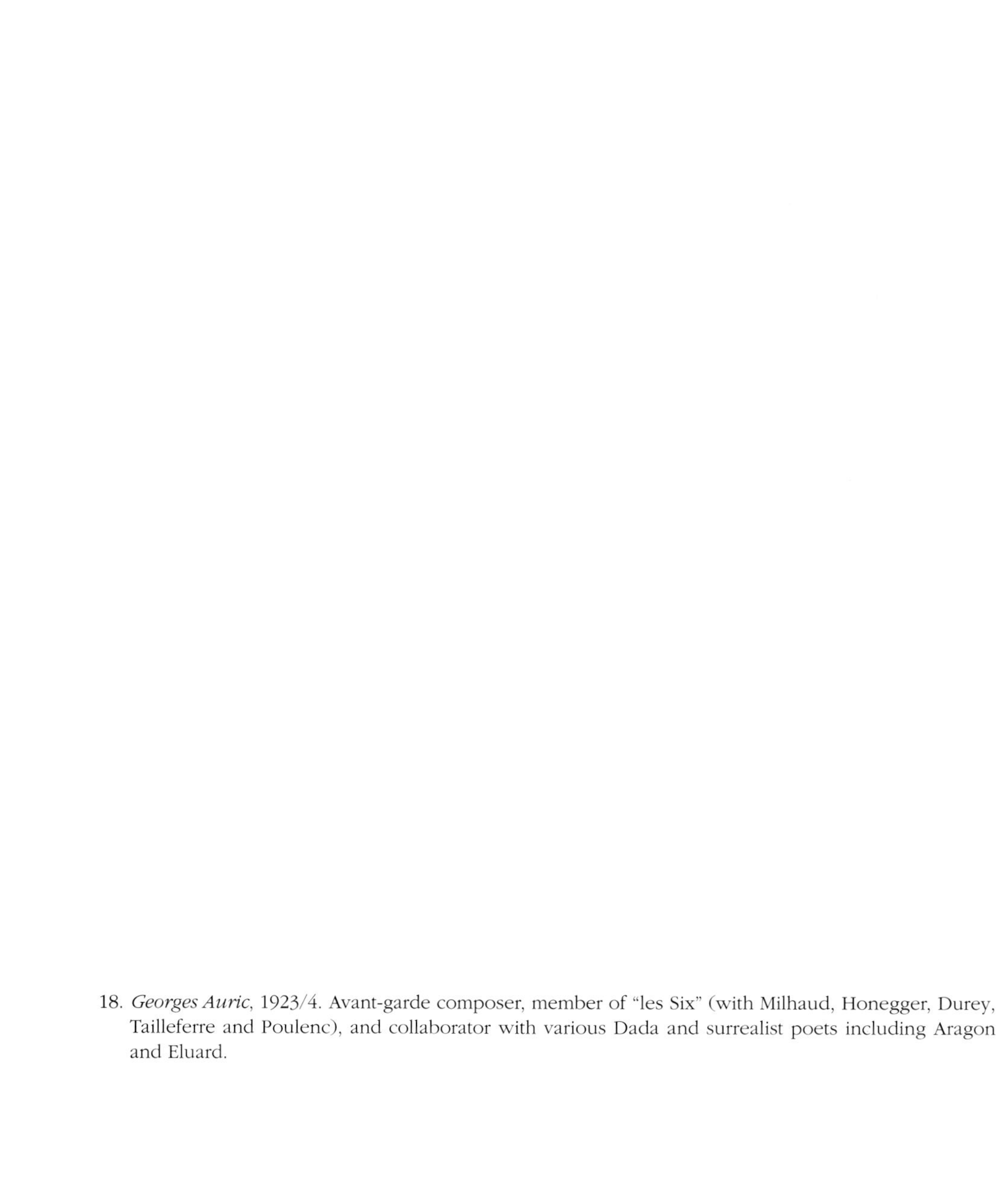

18. *Georges Auric*, 1923/4. Avant-garde composer, member of "les Six" (with Milhaud, Honegger, Durey, Tailleferre and Poulenc), and collaborator with various Dada and surrealist poets including Aragon and Eluard.

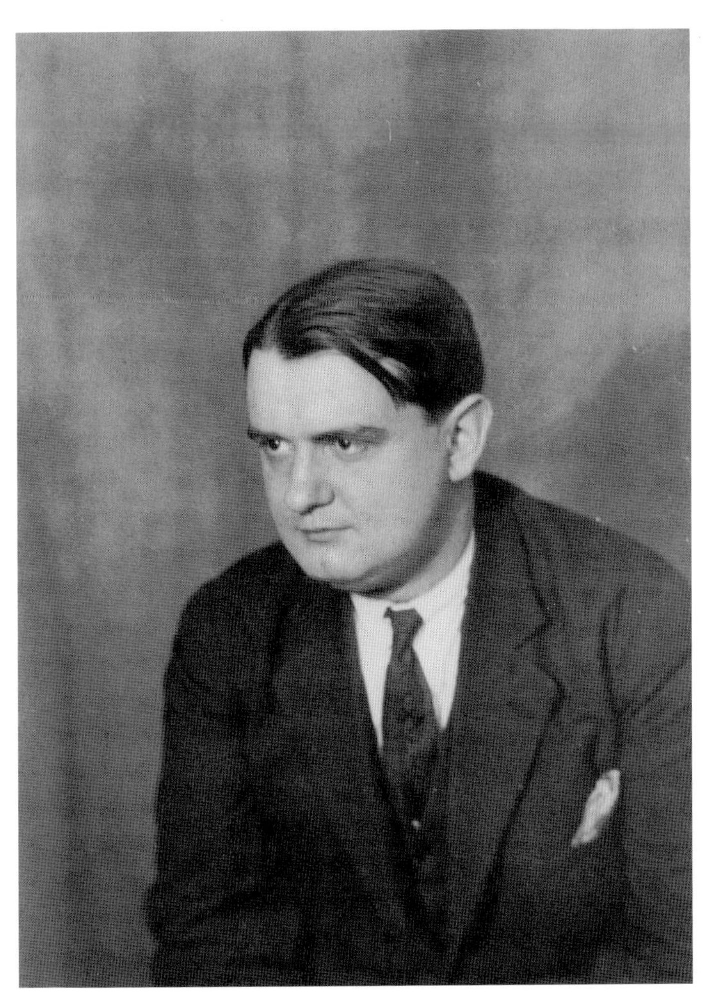

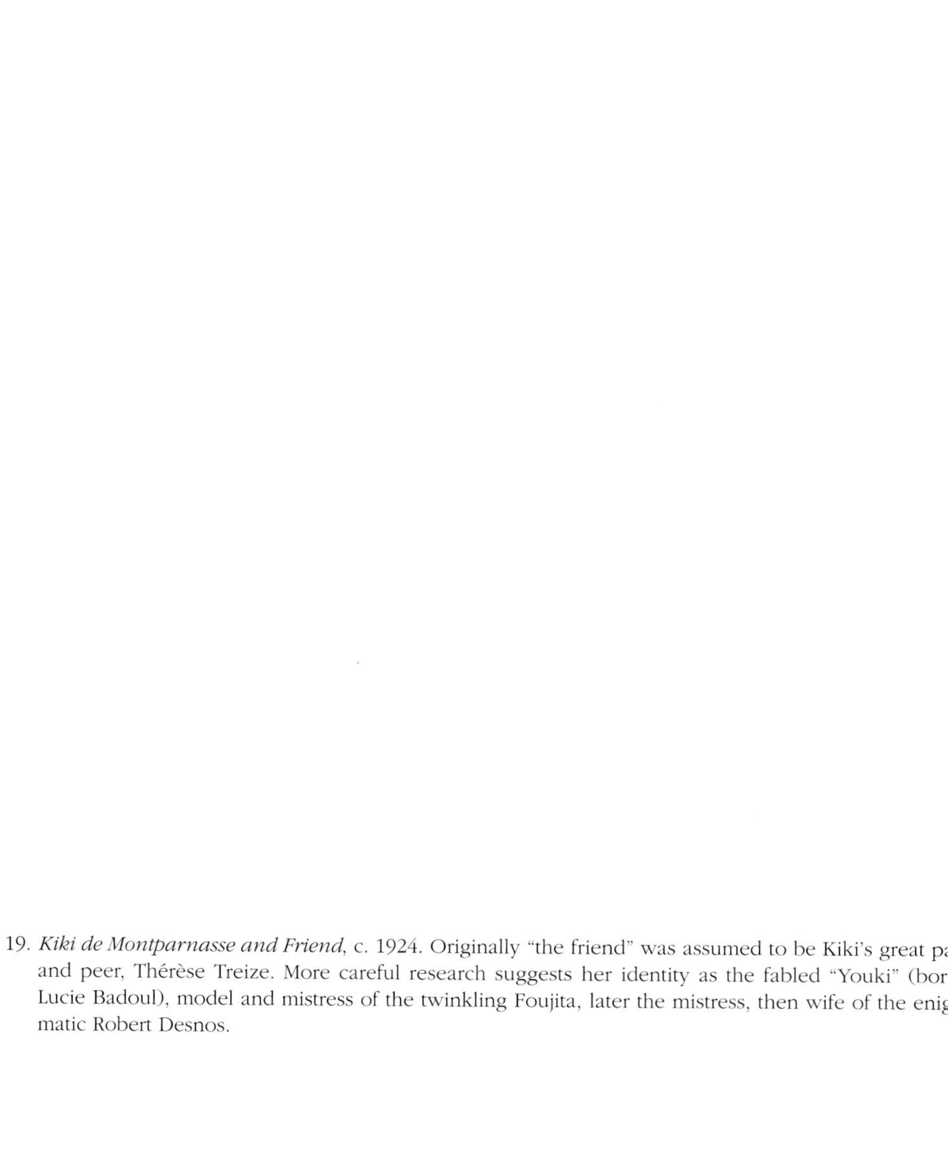

19. *Kiki de Montparnasse and Friend*, c. 1924. Originally "the friend" was assumed to be Kiki's great pal and peer, Thérèse Treize. More careful research suggests her identity as the fabled "Youki" (born Lucie Badoul), model and mistress of the twinkling Foujita, later the mistress, then wife of the enigmatic Robert Desnos.

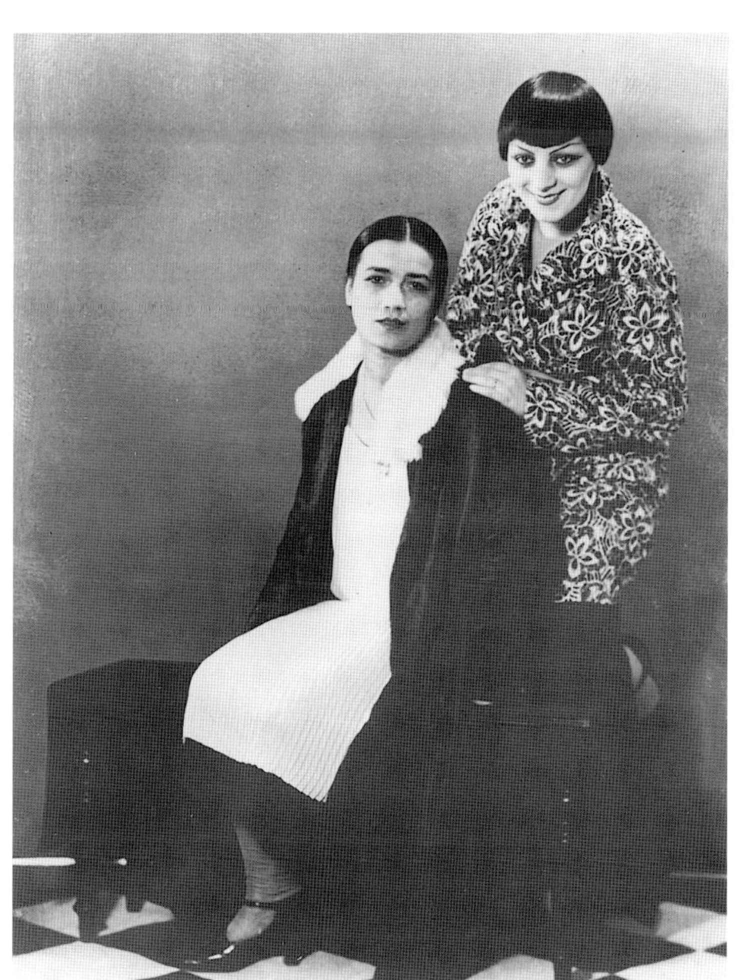

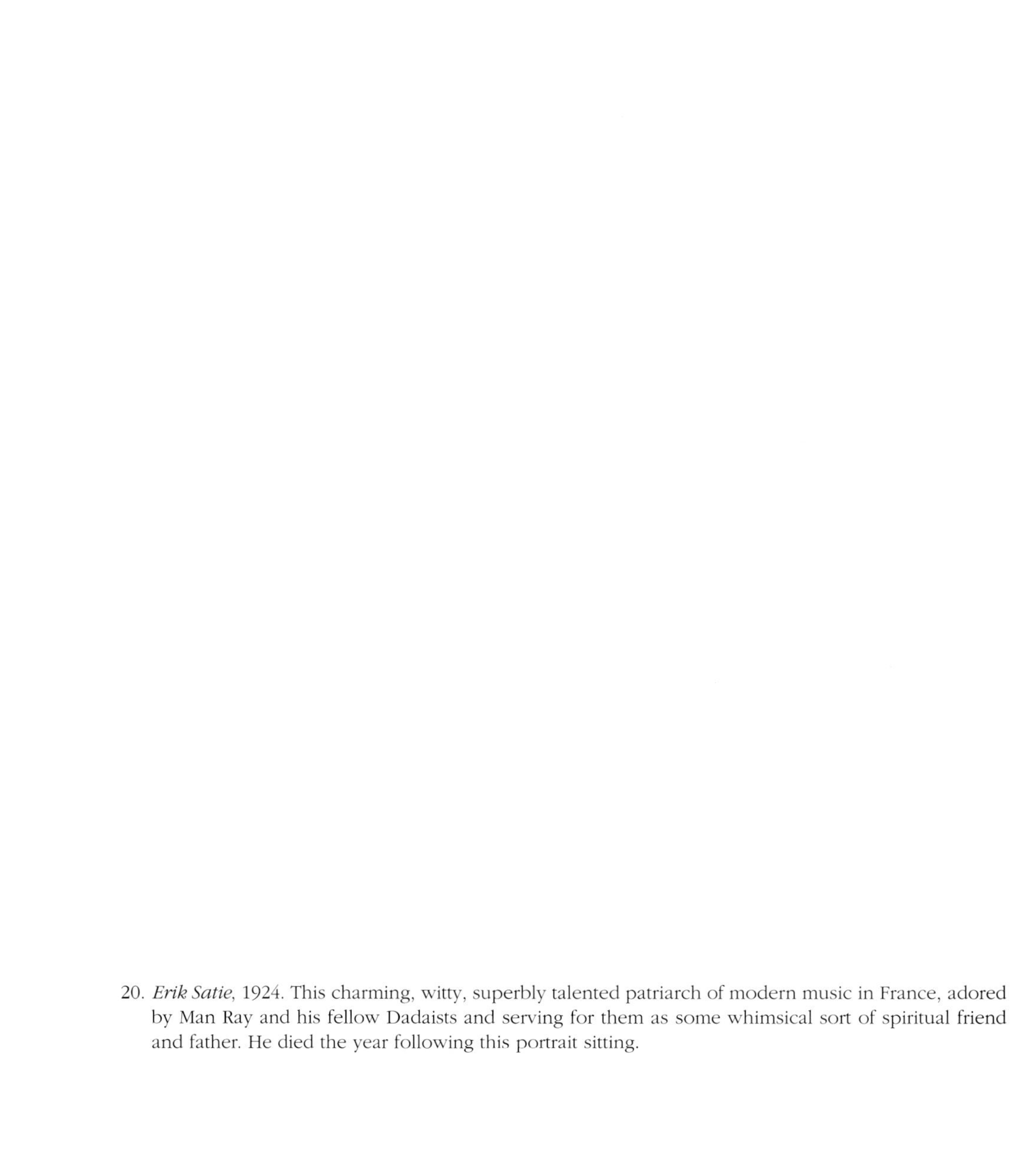

20. *Erik Satie*, 1924. This charming, witty, superbly talented patriarch of modern music in France, adored by Man Ray and his fellow Dadaists and serving for them as some whimsical sort of spiritual friend and father. He died the year following this portrait sitting.

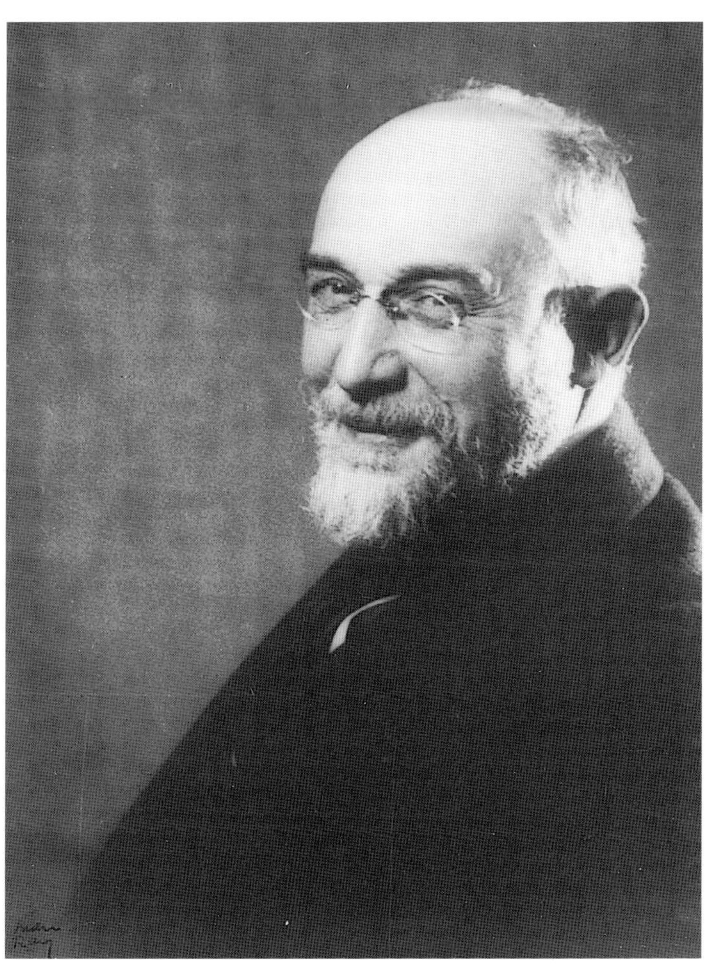

21. *Barbette*, 1924. Actual name: Vander Clyde; Place of birth: Round Rock, Texas. "Artiste suprême" of the high wire and trapeze, both in circuses and the greatest nightclubs and cabarets of the day, always in superb, exquisite female costume, always divulging the secret of his identity with muscular torso bared and wig in hand at the end of the performance.

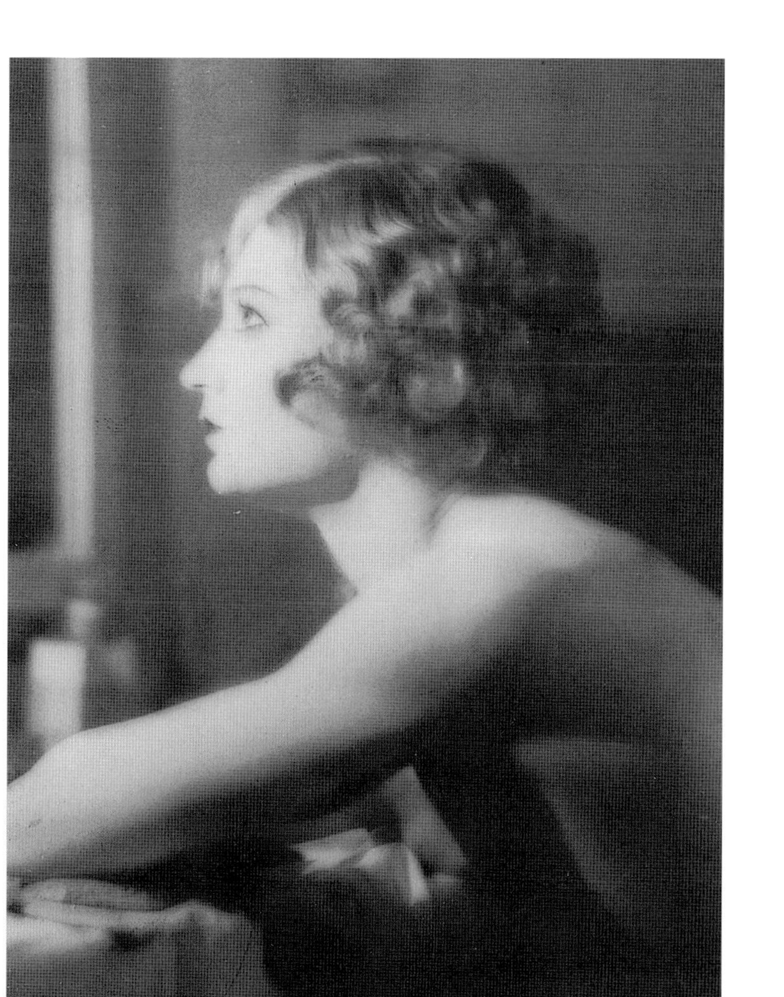

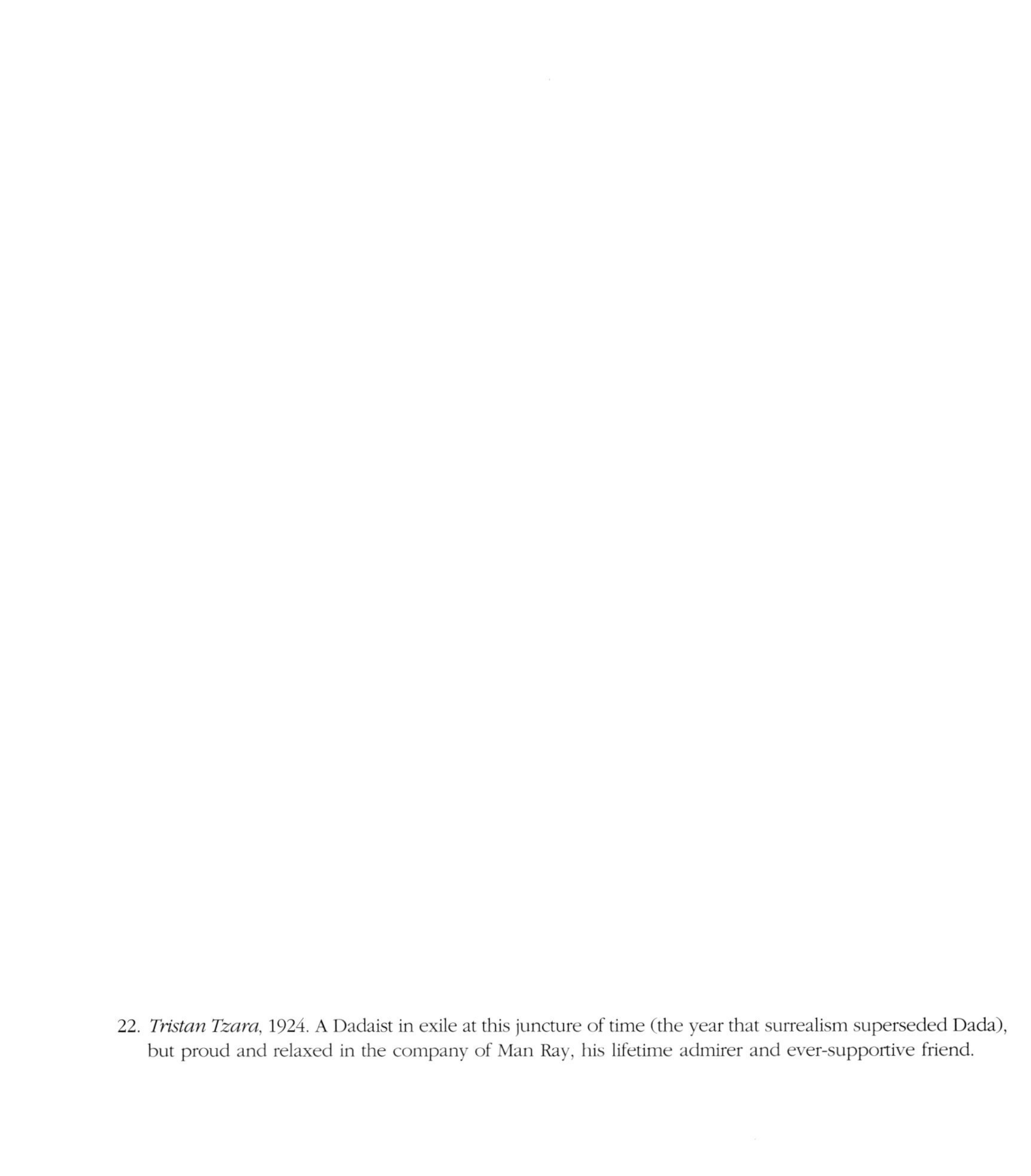

22. *Tristan Tzara*, 1924. A Dadaist in exile at this juncture of time (the year that surrealism superseded Dada), but proud and relaxed in the company of Man Ray, his lifetime admirer and ever-supportive friend.

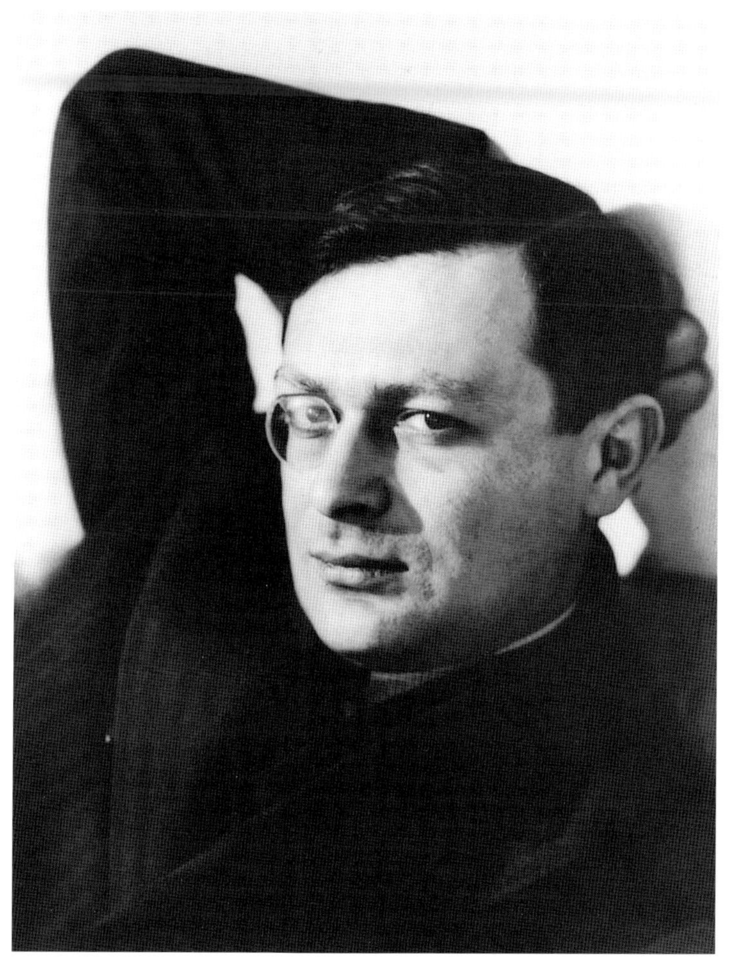

23. *Self-Portrait*, 1924. Probably the most formal and appealing of all of Man Ray's self-portraits: stylishly elegant courtesy of his suddenly-evolved success as a major fashion photographer; faintly confounded by the diminishment of his cherished activities as artist and related carefree dalliances with his Dada, now surrealist cronies.

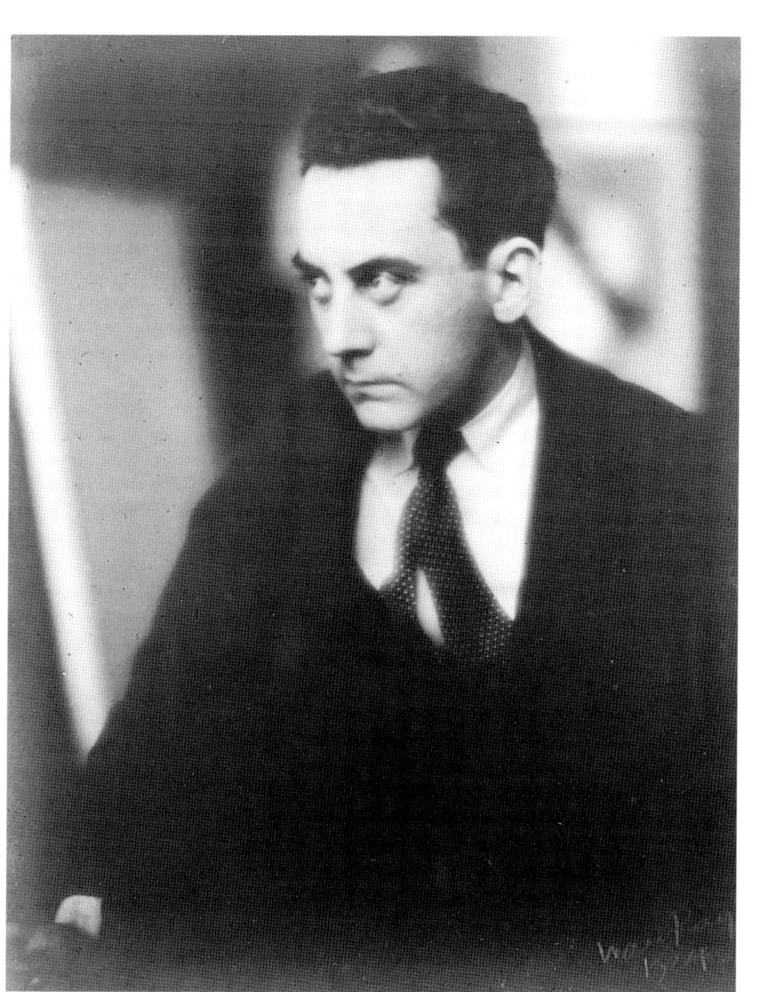

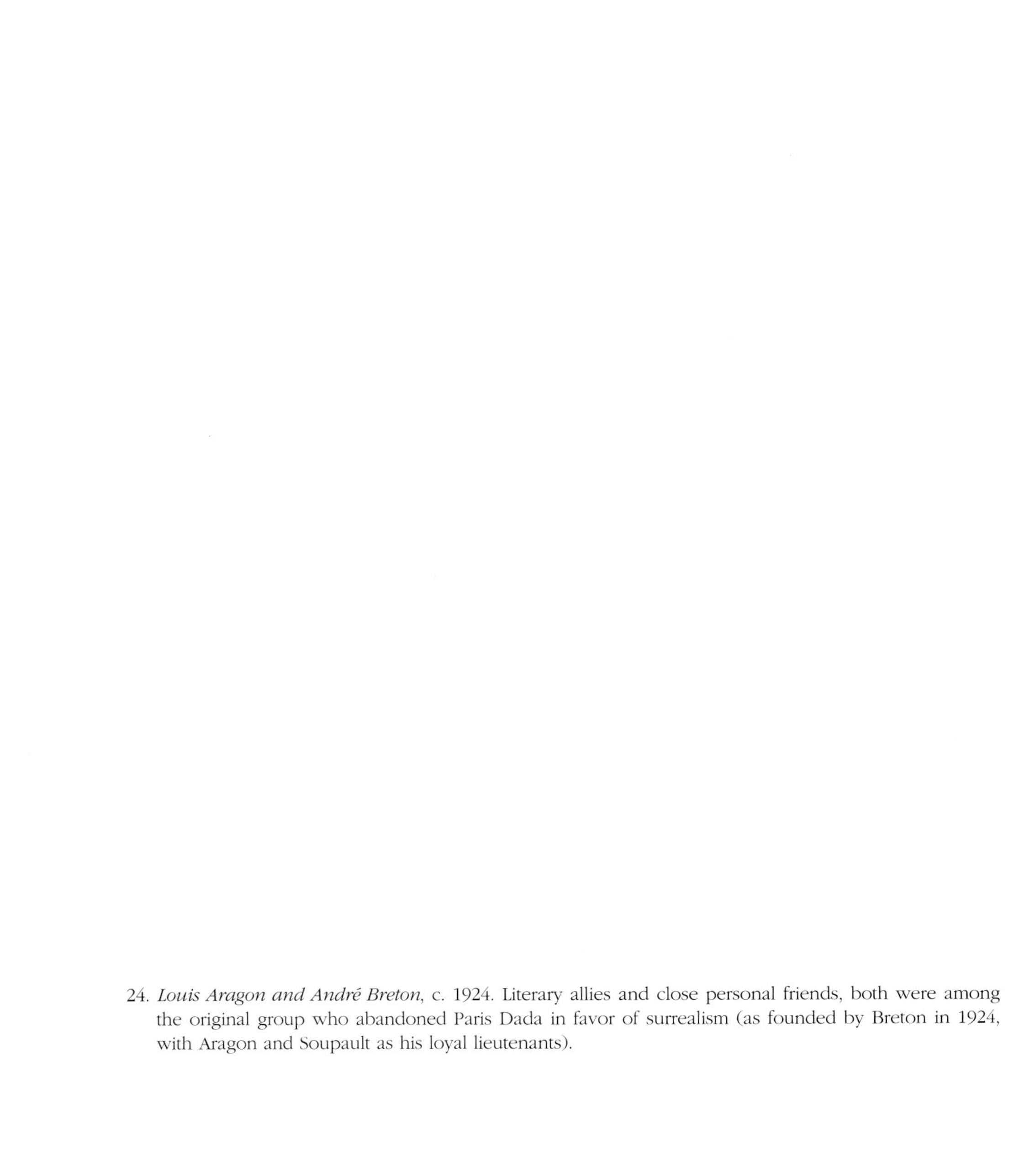

24. *Louis Aragon and André Breton*, c. 1924. Literary allies and close personal friends, both were among the original group who abandoned Paris Dada in favor of surrealism (as founded by Breton in 1924, with Aragon and Soupault as his loyal lieutenants).

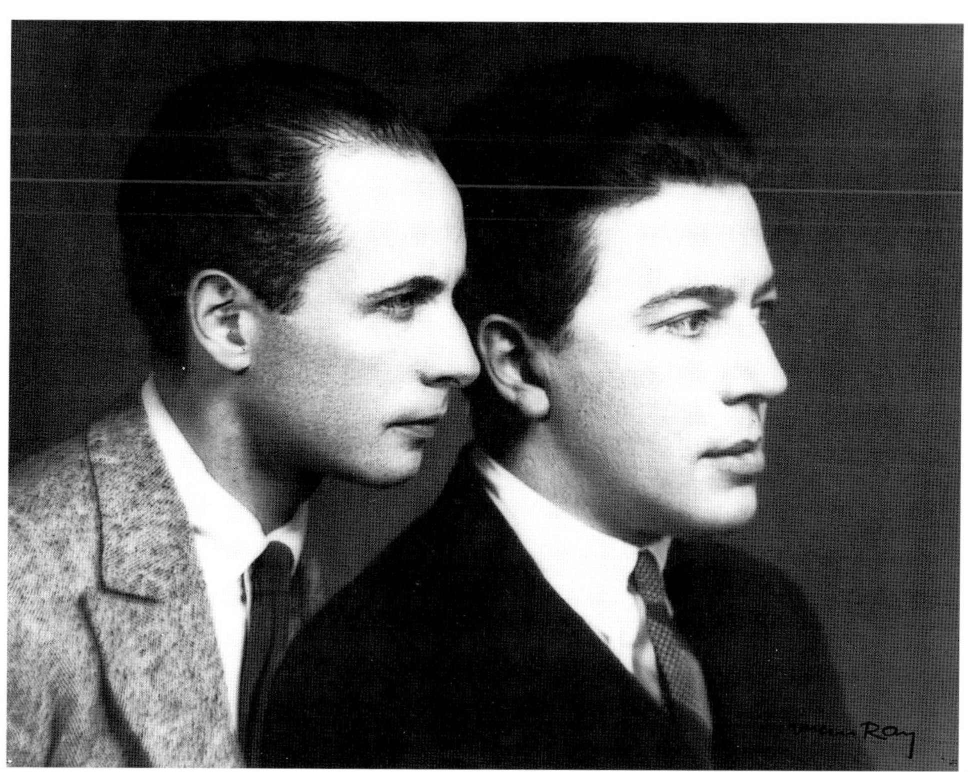

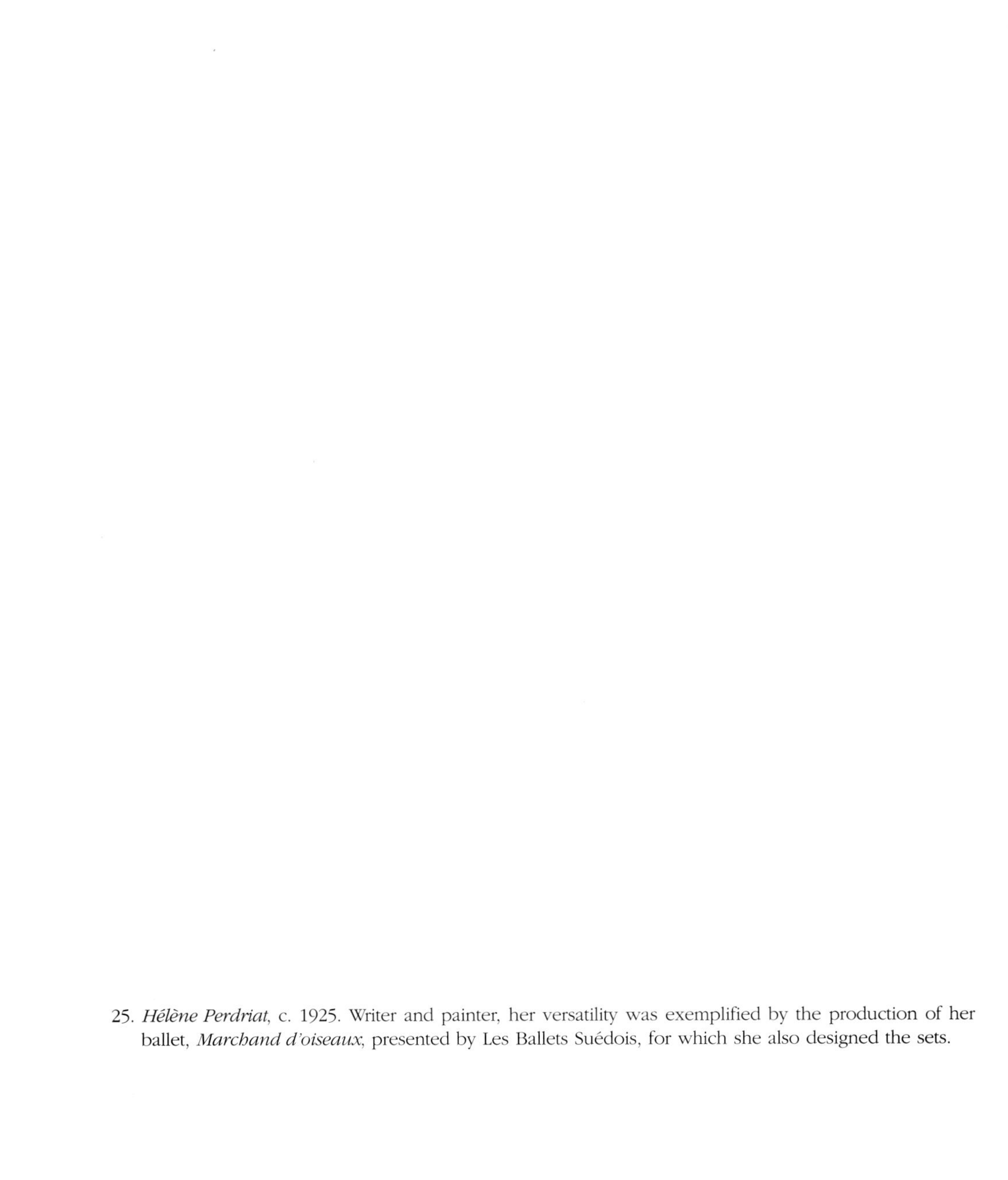

25. *Hélène Perdriat*, c. 1925. Writer and painter, her versatility was exemplified by the production of her ballet, *Marchand d'oiseaux*, presented by Les Ballets Suédois, for which she also designed the sets.

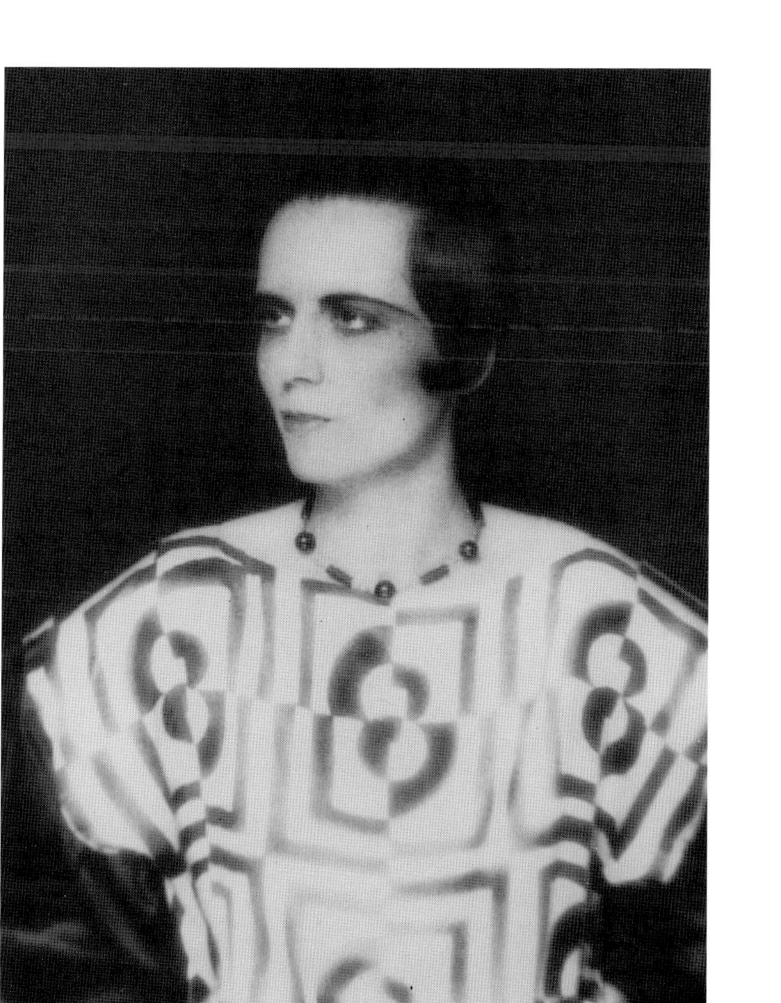

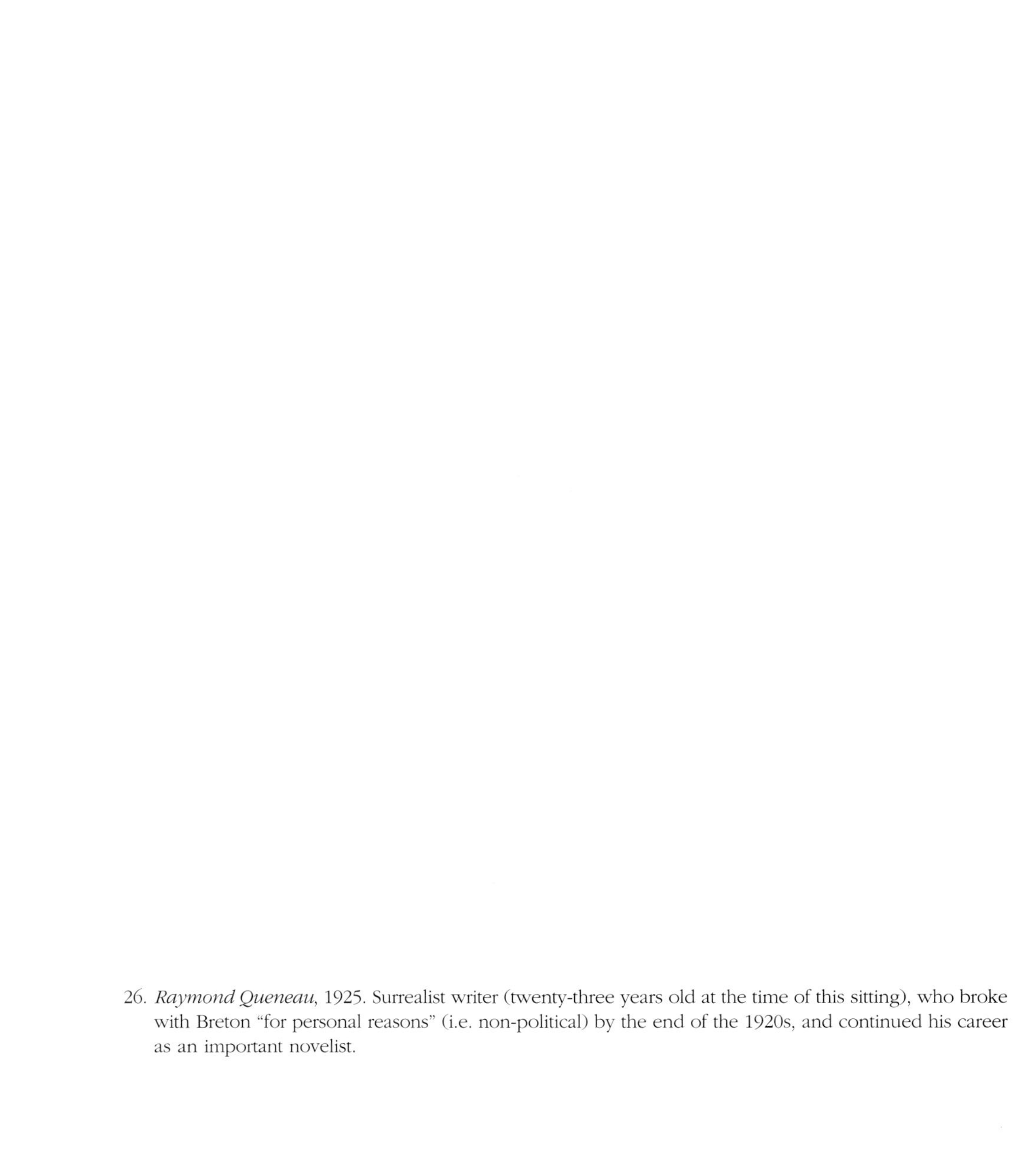

26. *Raymond Queneau*, 1925. Surrealist writer (twenty-three years old at the time of this sitting), who broke with Breton "for personal reasons" (i.e. non-political) by the end of the 1920s, and continued his career as an important novelist.

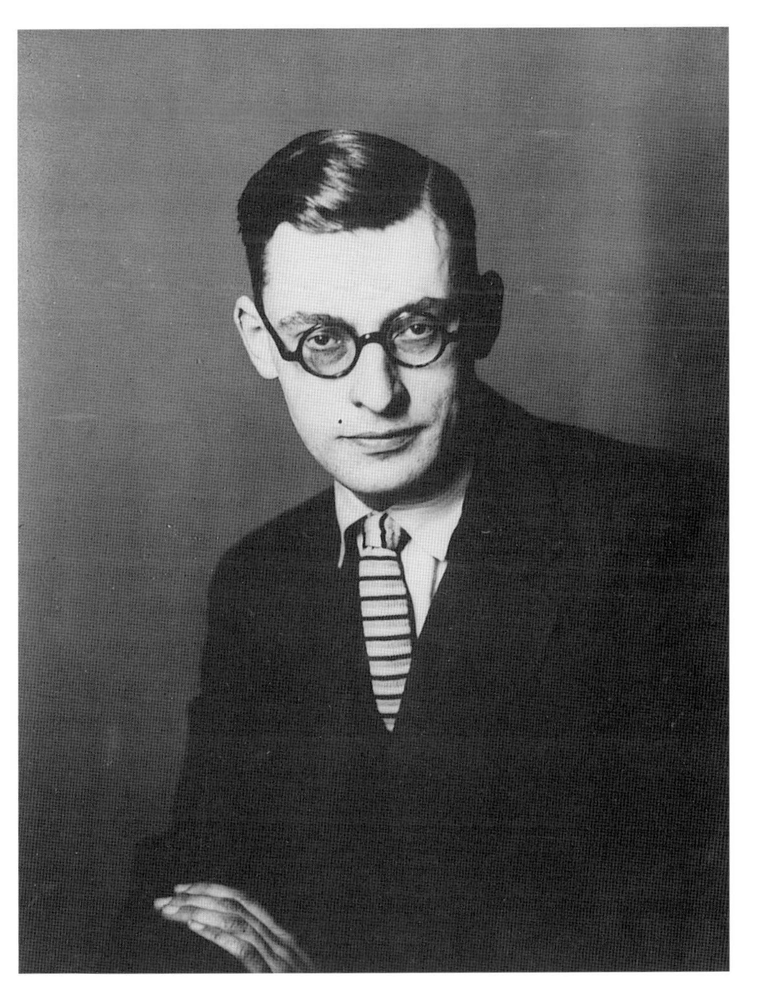

27. *Janine*, 1924/5. Described on a label affixed to verso: "JANINE, one of PATOU's French mannequins, wearing a day ensemble for Spring, 1925...Please credit MAN RAY." Business, as pleasure.

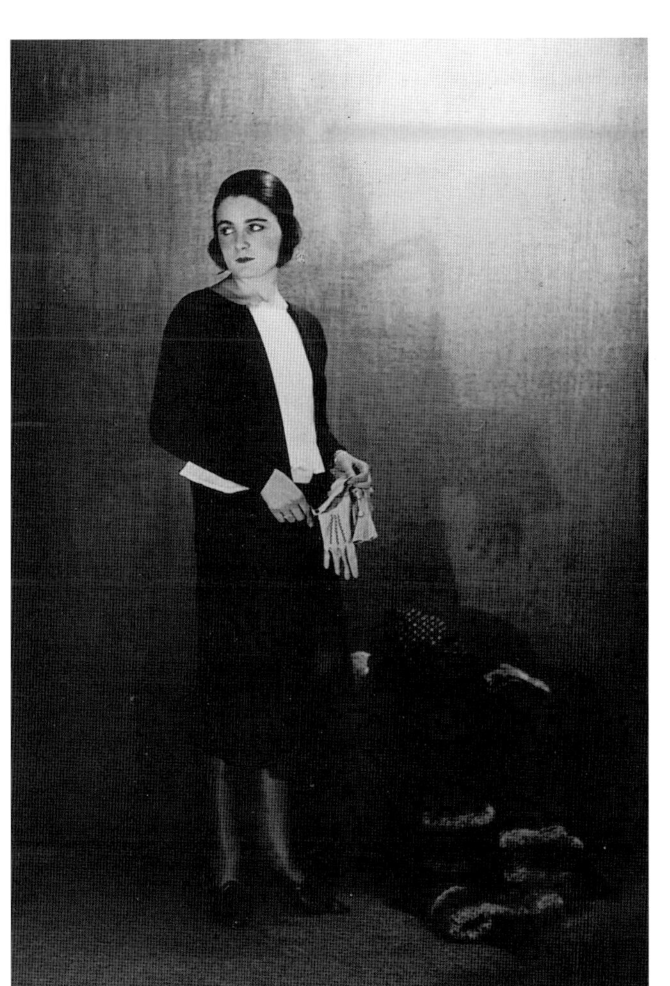

28. *René Crevel*, c. 1925. The "enfant terrible" of the surrealist poets, he was regarded by Breton as an "ultimate surrealist". When he chose to take his life at the age of thirty-five, he left behind a note inscribed with a single word: "Degouté".

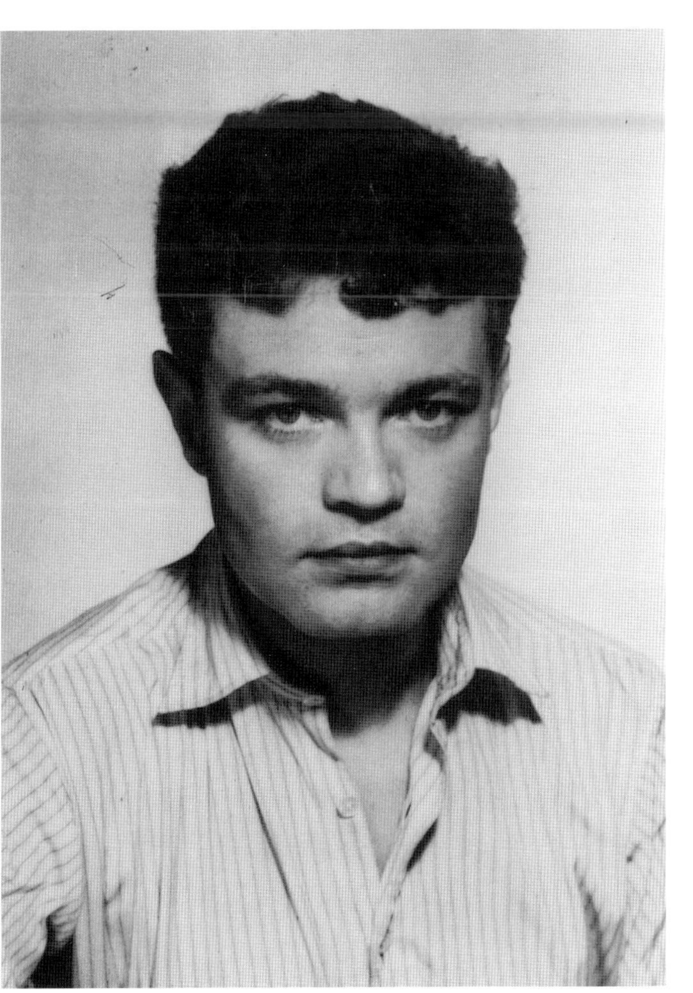

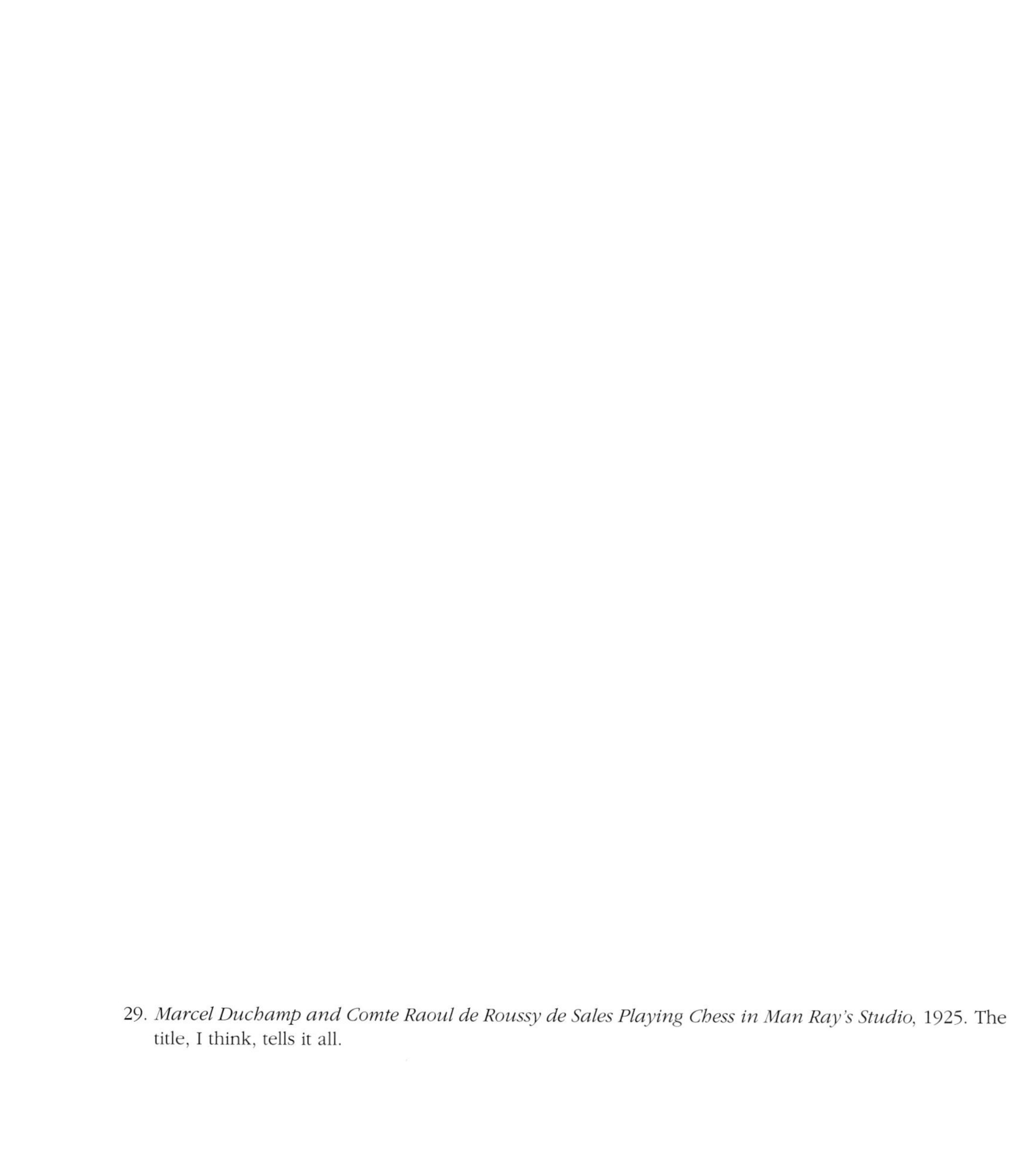

29. *Marcel Duchamp and Comte Raoul de Roussy de Sales Playing Chess in Man Ray's Studio*, 1925. The title, I think, tells it all.

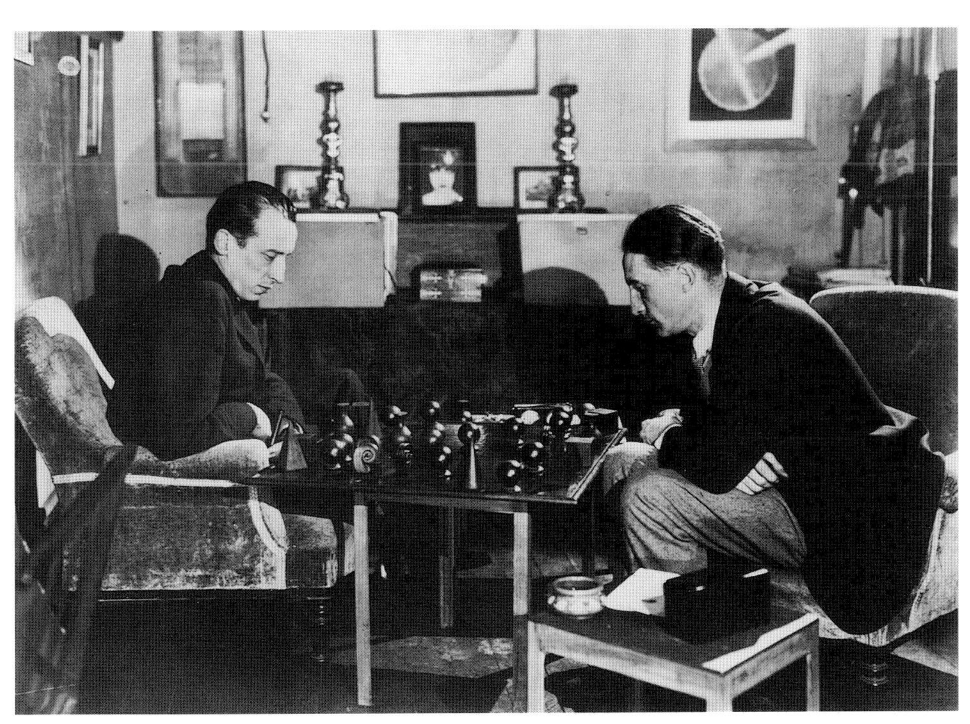

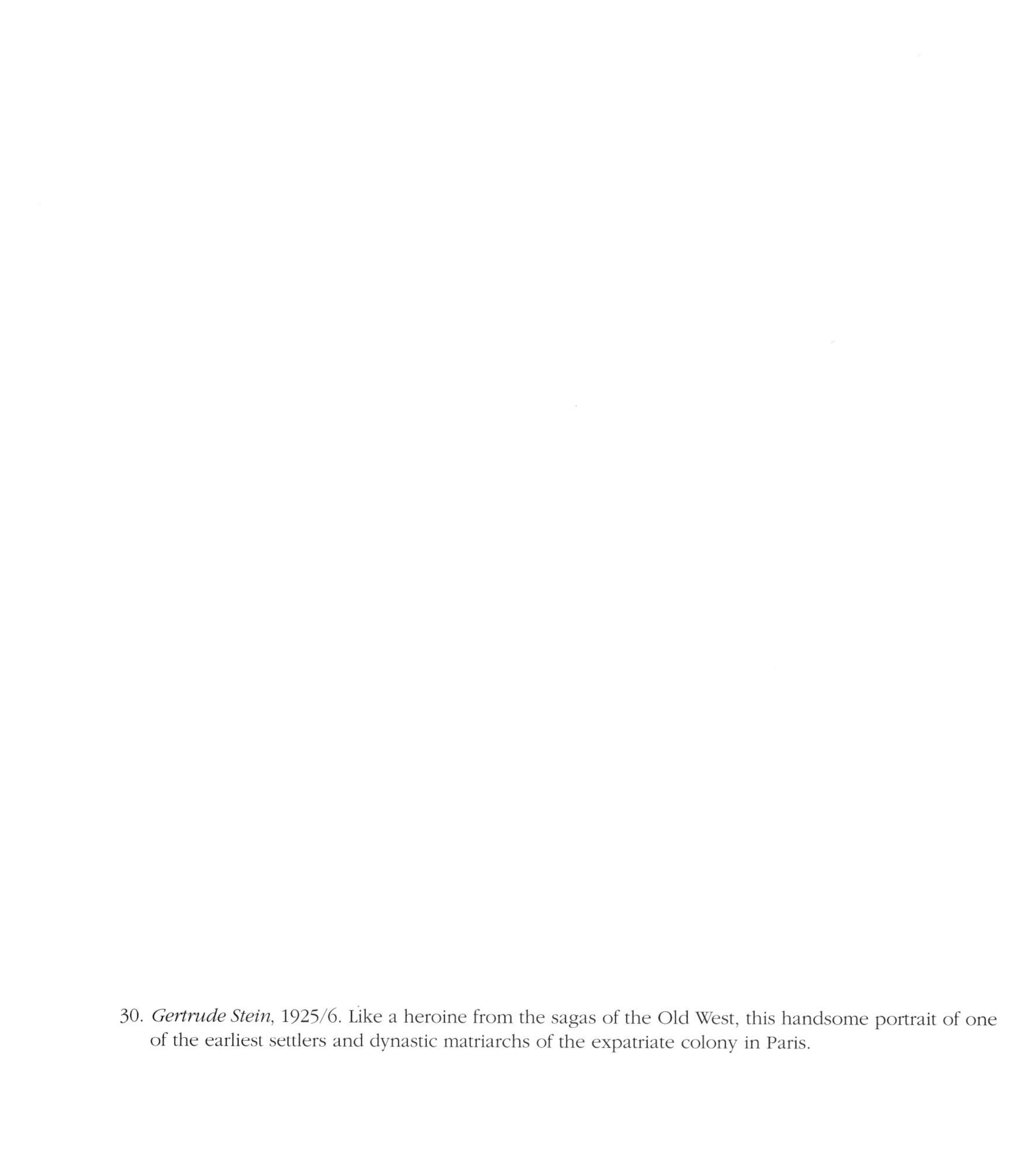

30. *Gertrude Stein*, 1925/6. Like a heroine from the sagas of the Old West, this handsome portrait of one of the earliest settlers and dynastic matriarchs of the expatriate colony in Paris.

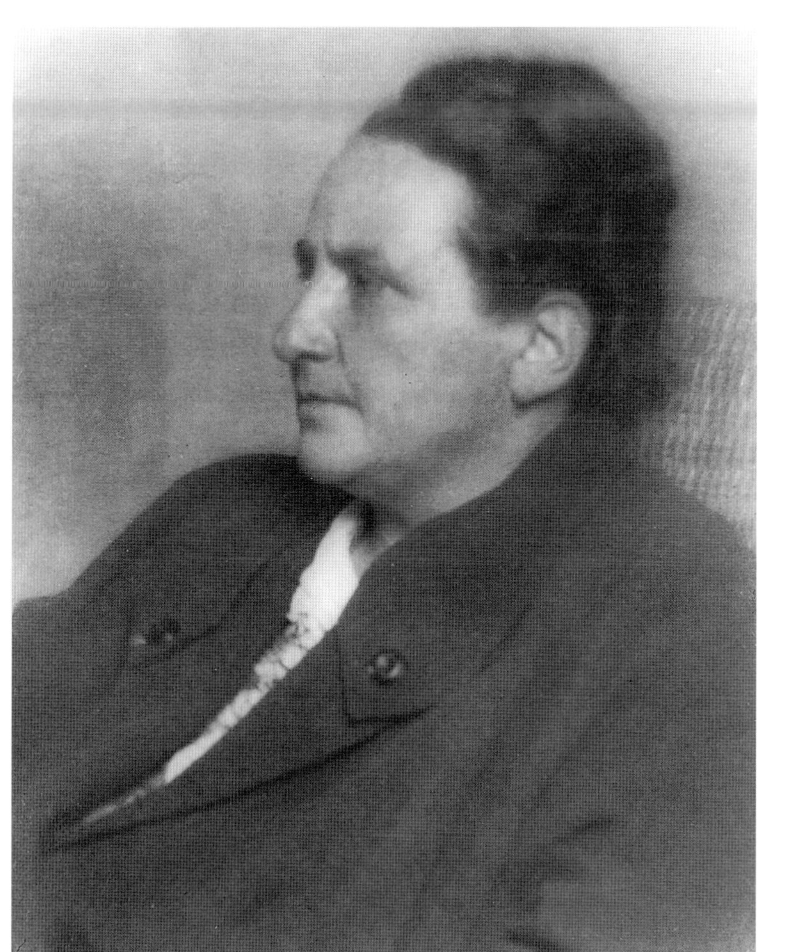

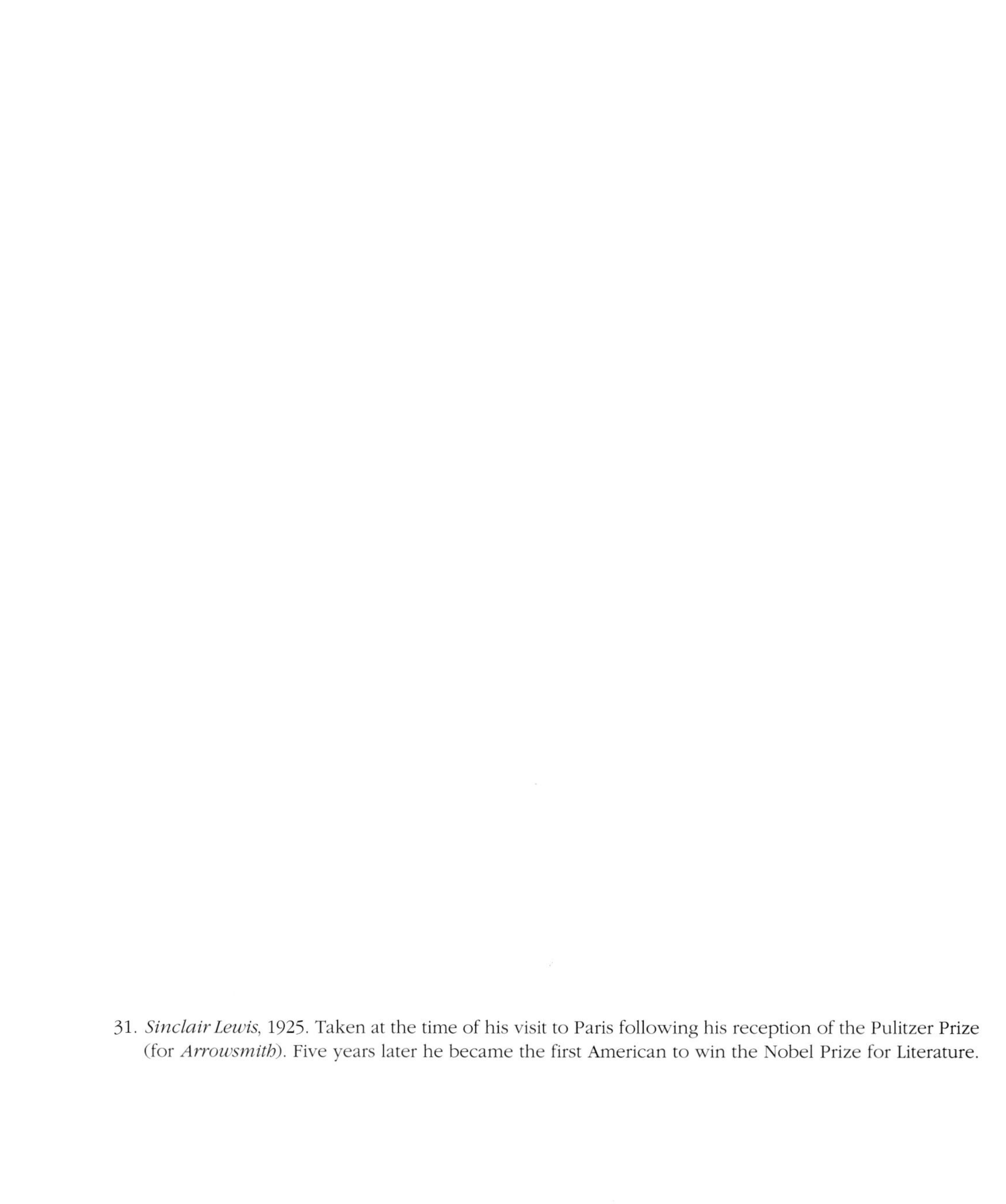

31. *Sinclair Lewis*, 1925. Taken at the time of his visit to Paris following his reception of the Pulitzer Prize (for *Arrowsmith*). Five years later he became the first American to win the Nobel Prize for Literature.

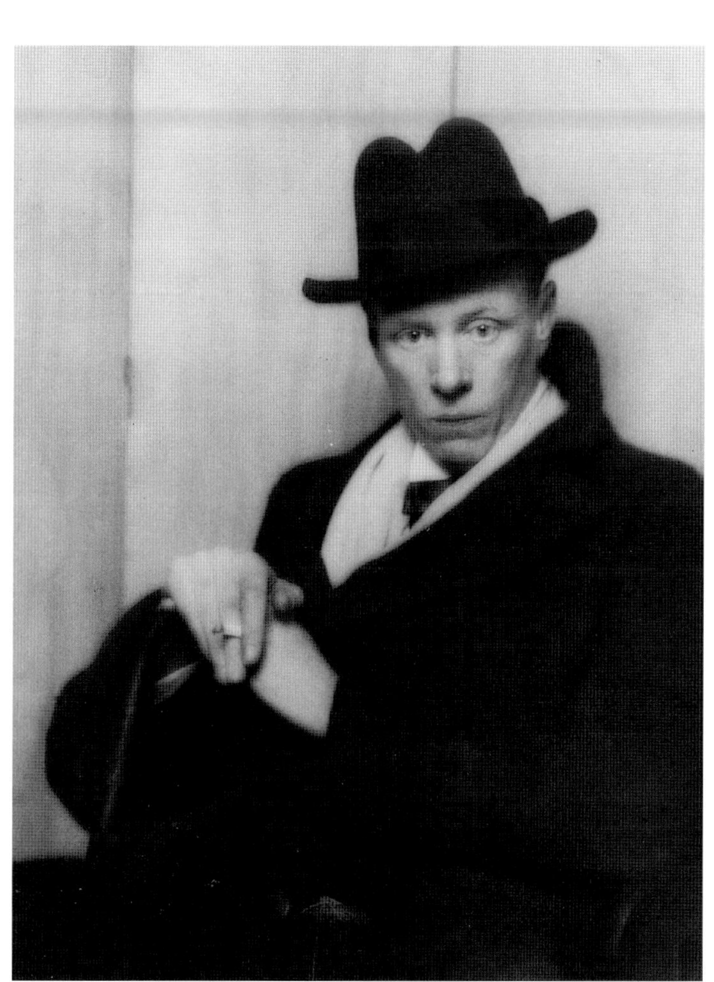

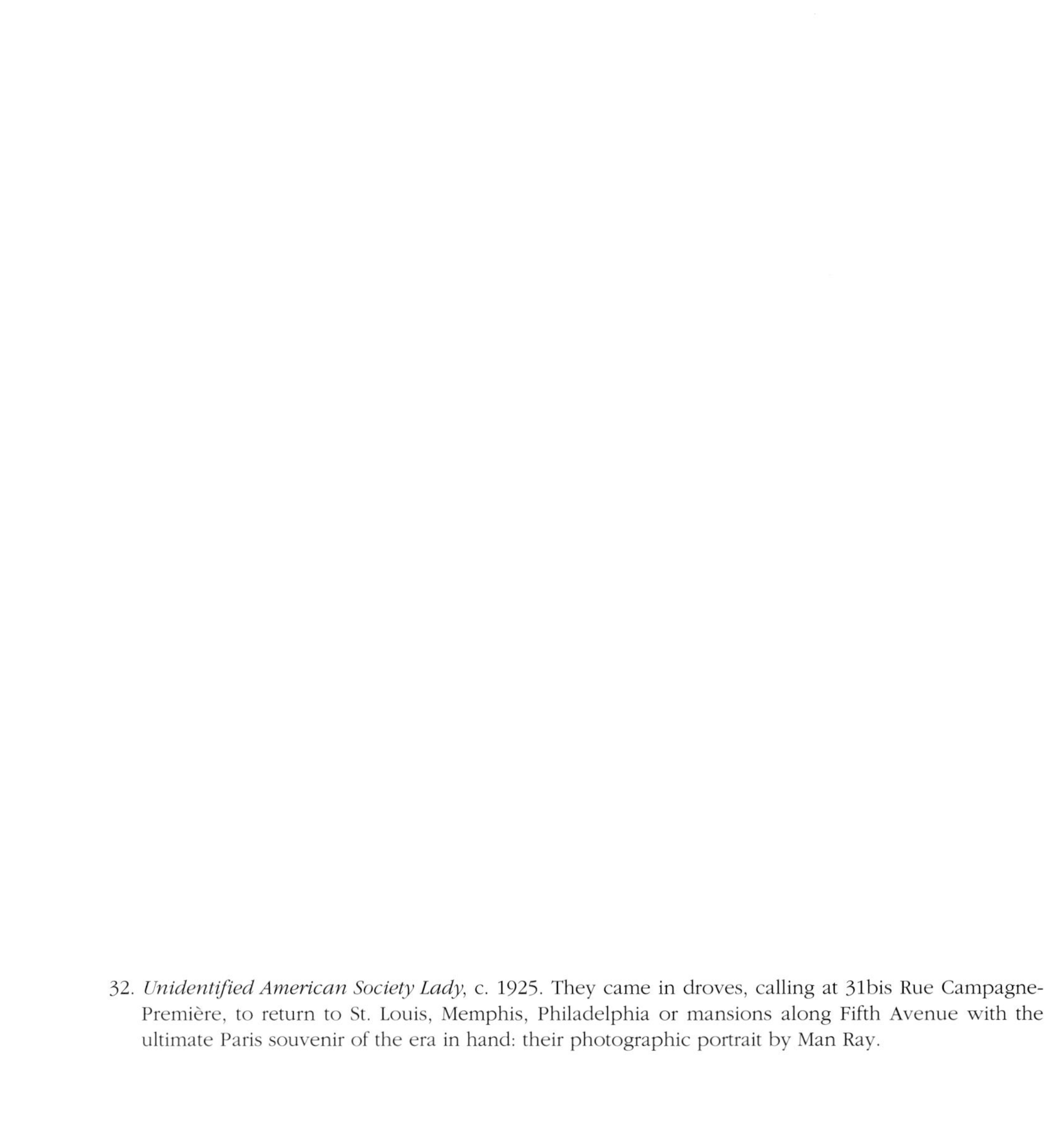

32. *Unidentified American Society Lady,* c. 1925. They came in droves, calling at 31bis Rue Campagne-Première, to return to St. Louis, Memphis, Philadelphia or mansions along Fifth Avenue with the ultimate Paris souvenir of the era in hand: their photographic portrait by Man Ray.

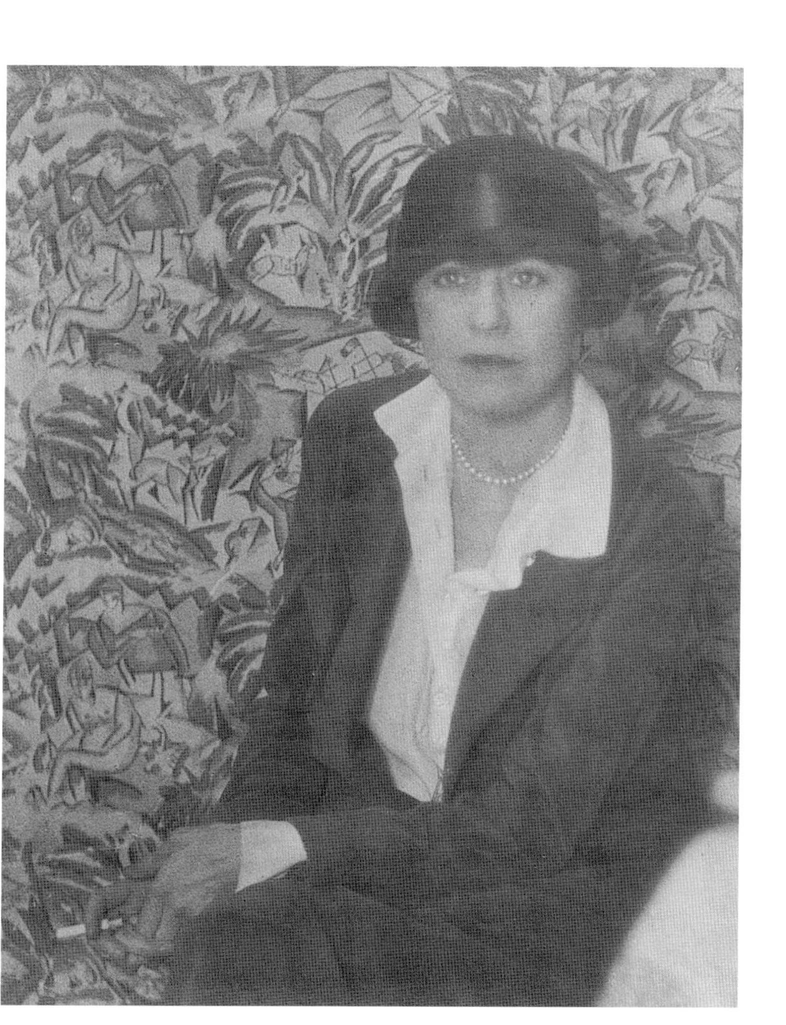

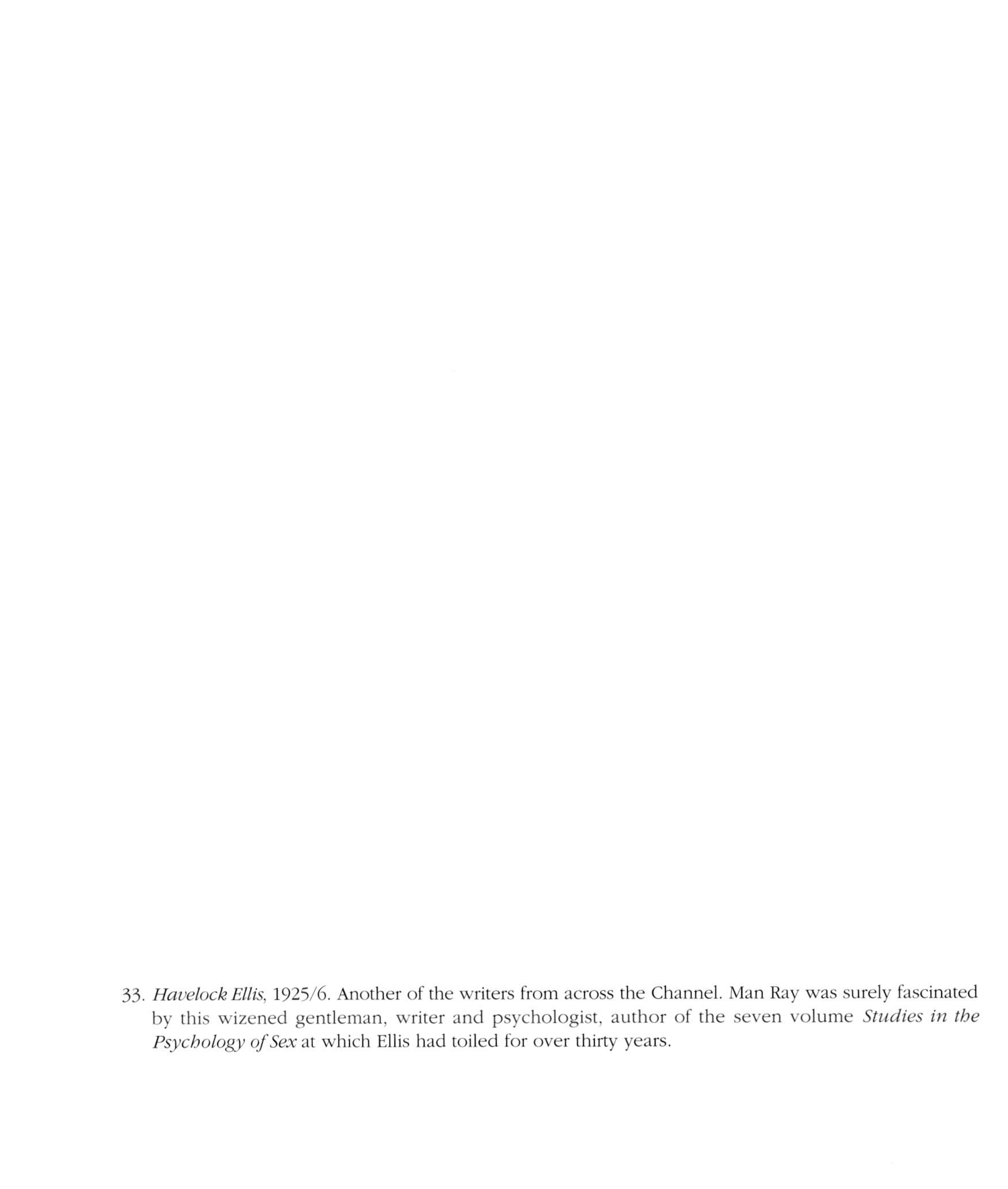

33. *Havelock Ellis*, 1925/6. Another of the writers from across the Channel. Man Ray was surely fascinated by this wizened gentleman, writer and psychologist, author of the seven volume *Studies in the Psychology of Sex* at which Ellis had toiled for over thirty years.

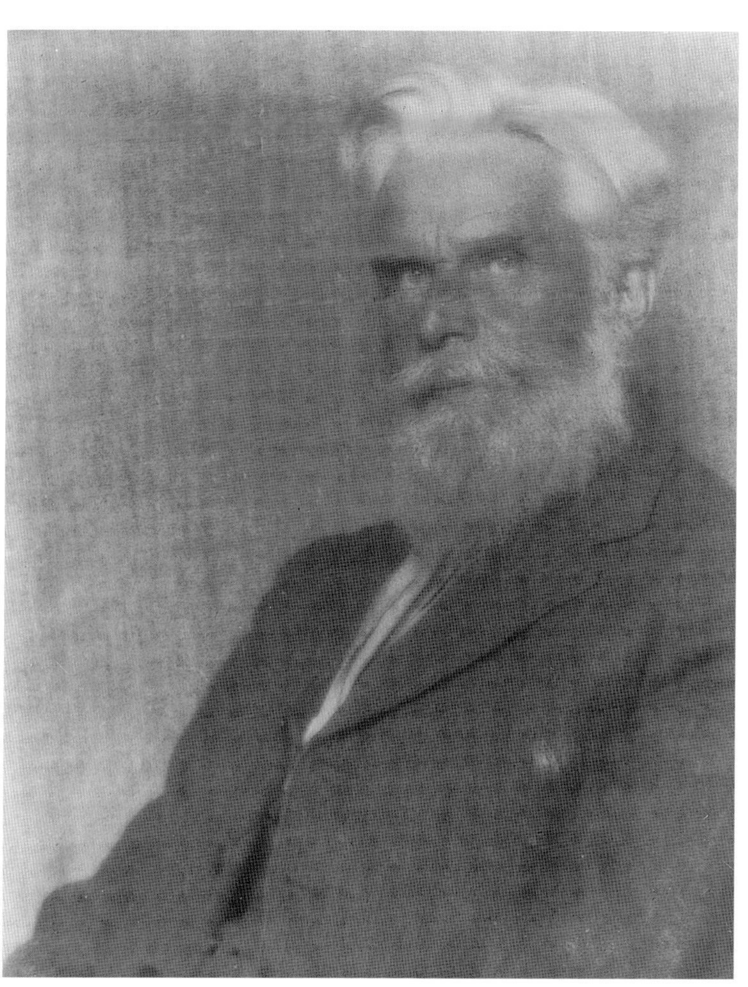

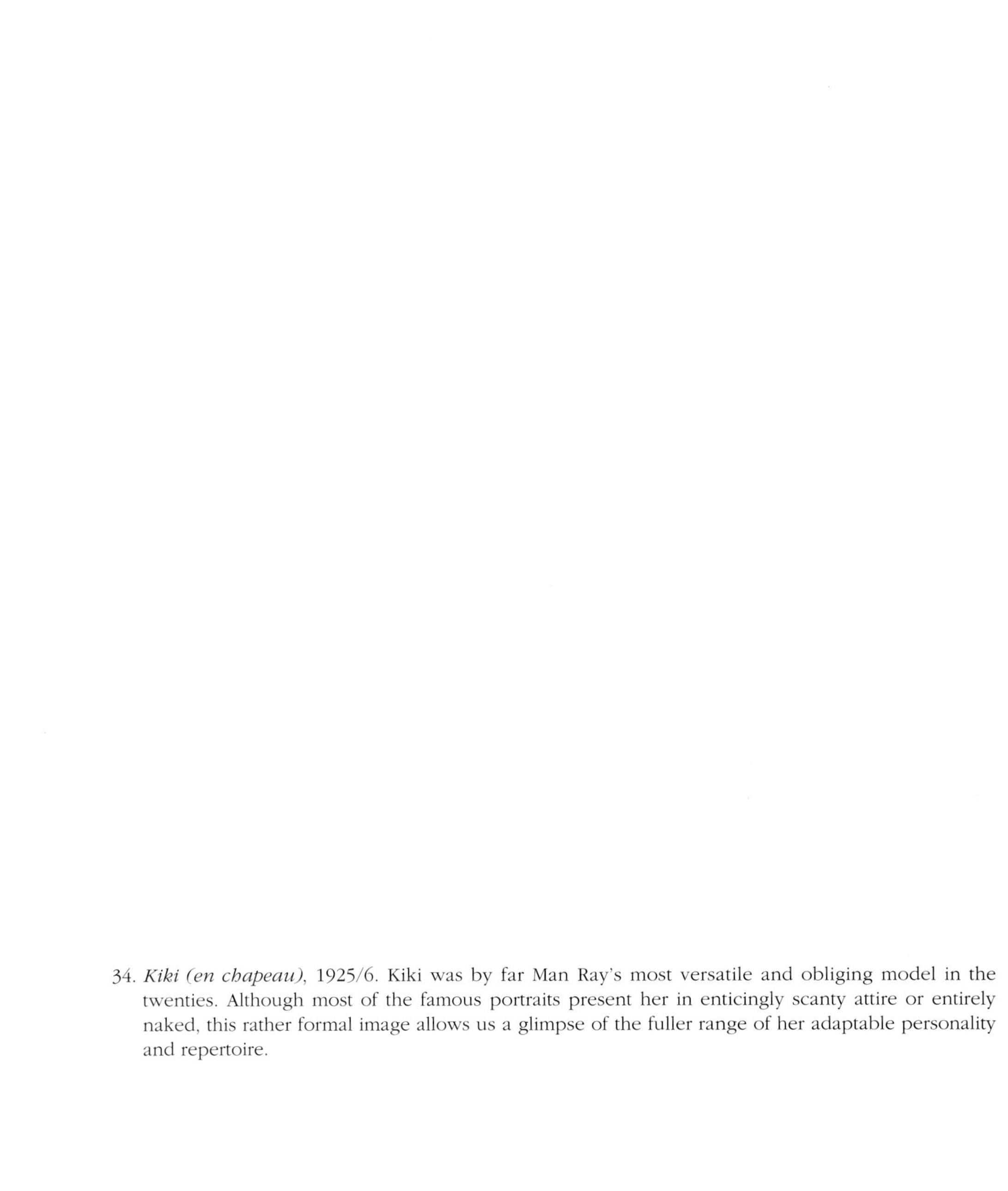

34. *Kiki (en chapeau)*, 1925/6. Kiki was by far Man Ray's most versatile and obliging model in the twenties. Although most of the famous portraits present her in enticingly scanty attire or entirely naked, this rather formal image allows us a glimpse of the fuller range of her adaptable personality and repertoire.

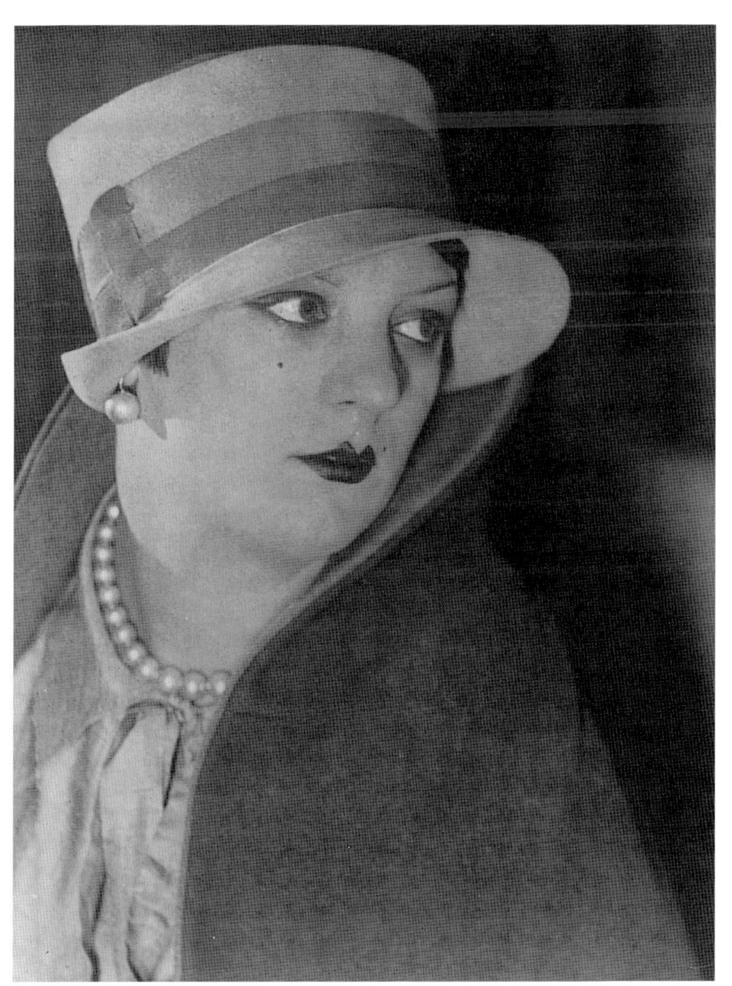

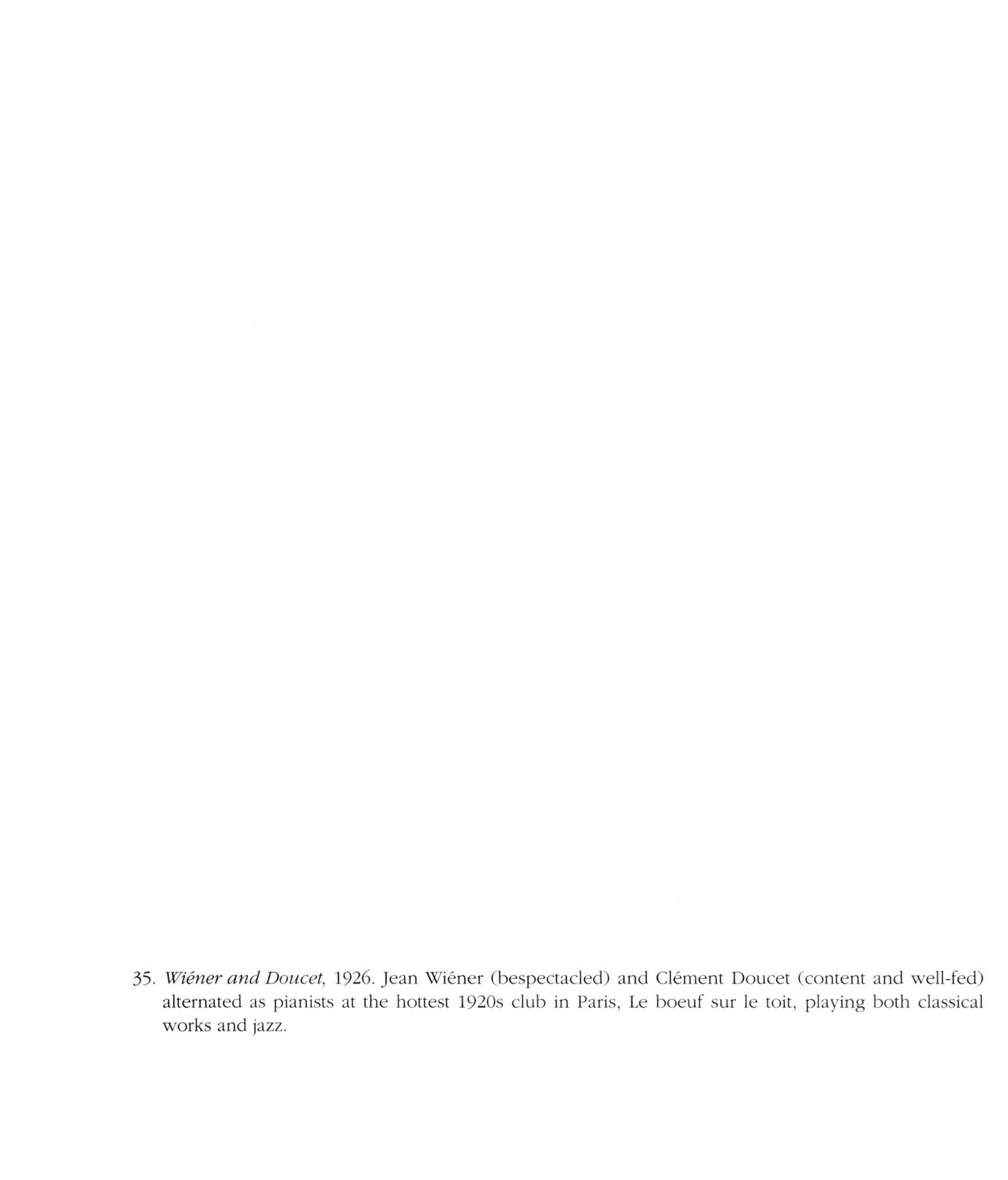

35. *Wiéner and Doucet,* 1926. Jean Wiéner (bespectacled) and Clément Doucet (content and well-fed) alternated as pianists at the hottest 1920s club in Paris, Le boeuf sur le toit, playing both classical works and jazz.

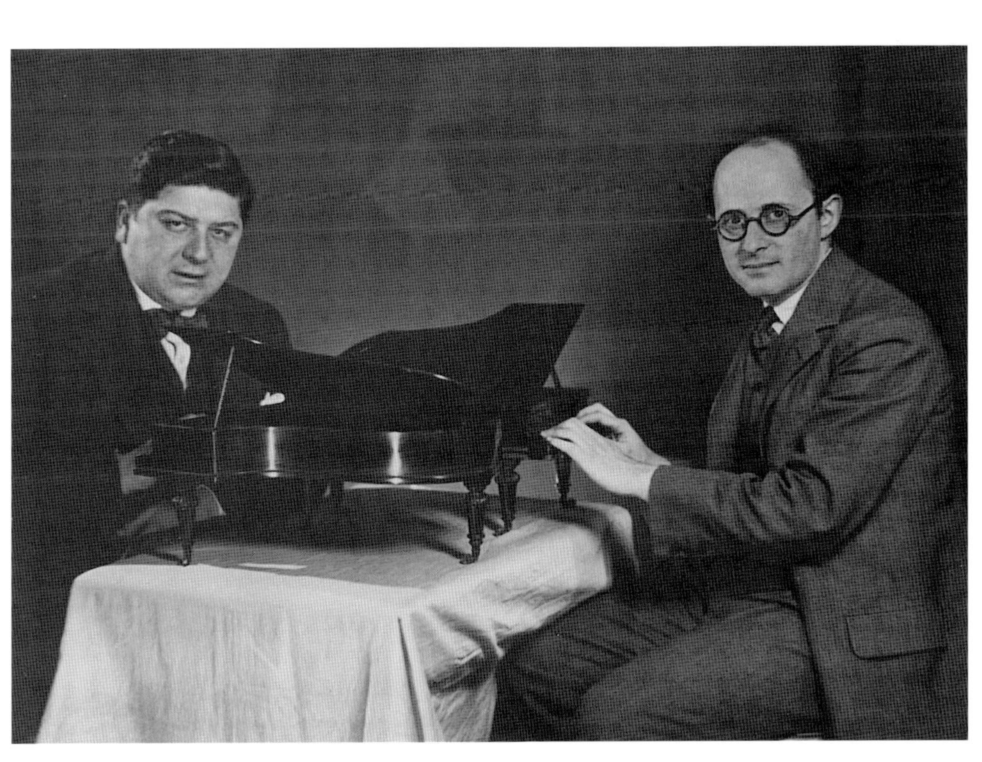

36. *Kay Boyle*, c. 1926. American expatriate short story writer “par excellence”.

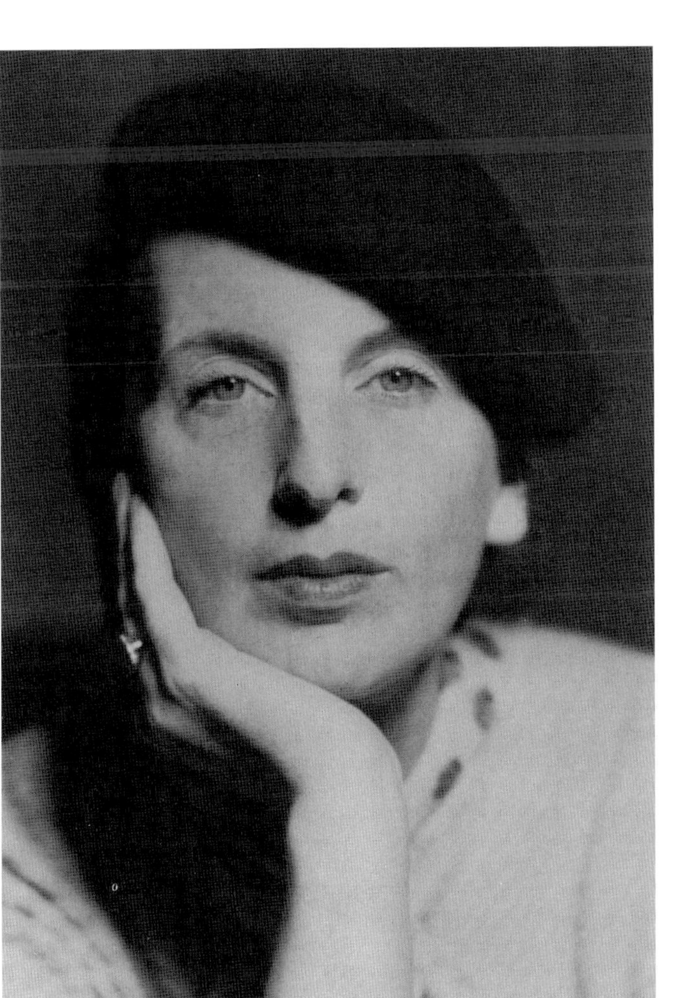

37. *Joan Miró*, 1926 (or early 1930s?). Almost every book that cites this famous photograph dates it as 1930 or 1933. After conferring with Billy Kluver and Julie Martin (co-authors of the marvelous *Kiki's Paris*), I'll go along with their well-researched approximation of 1926 (the year Max Ernst jokingly threatened to hang Miró with a thick-coiled rope if he didn't learn to become more conversational, in the presence of a highly amused Man Ray).

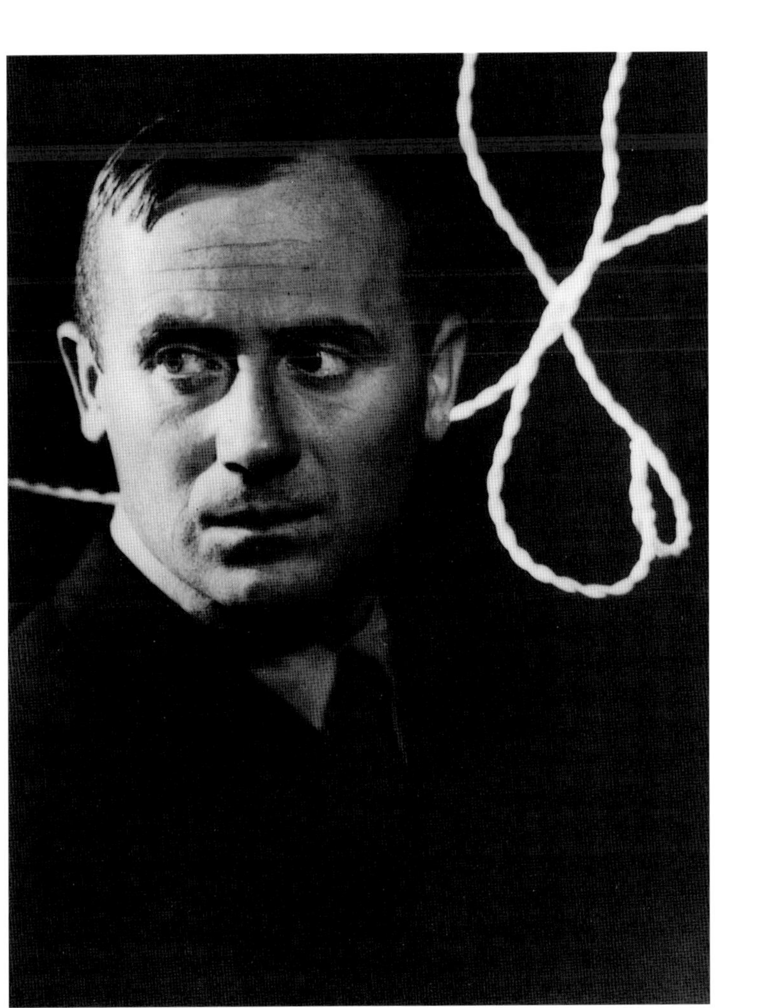

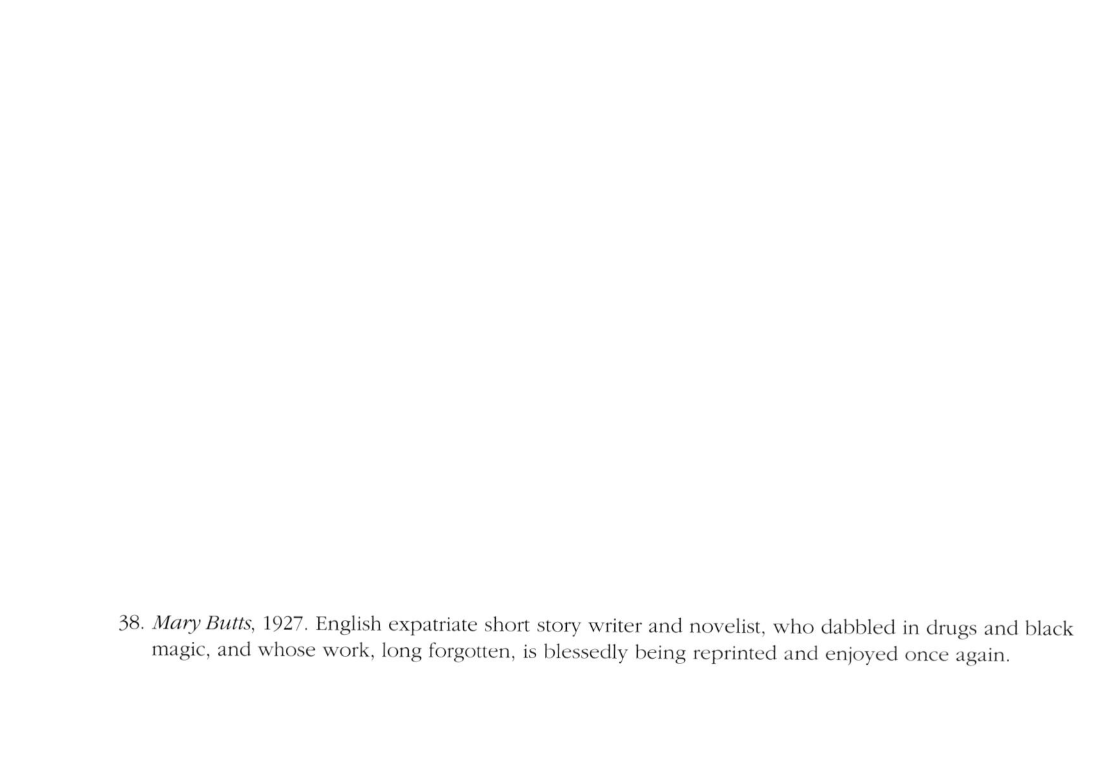

38. *Mary Butts*, 1927. English expatriate short story writer and novelist, who dabbled in drugs and black magic, and whose work, long forgotten, is blessedly being reprinted and enjoyed once again.

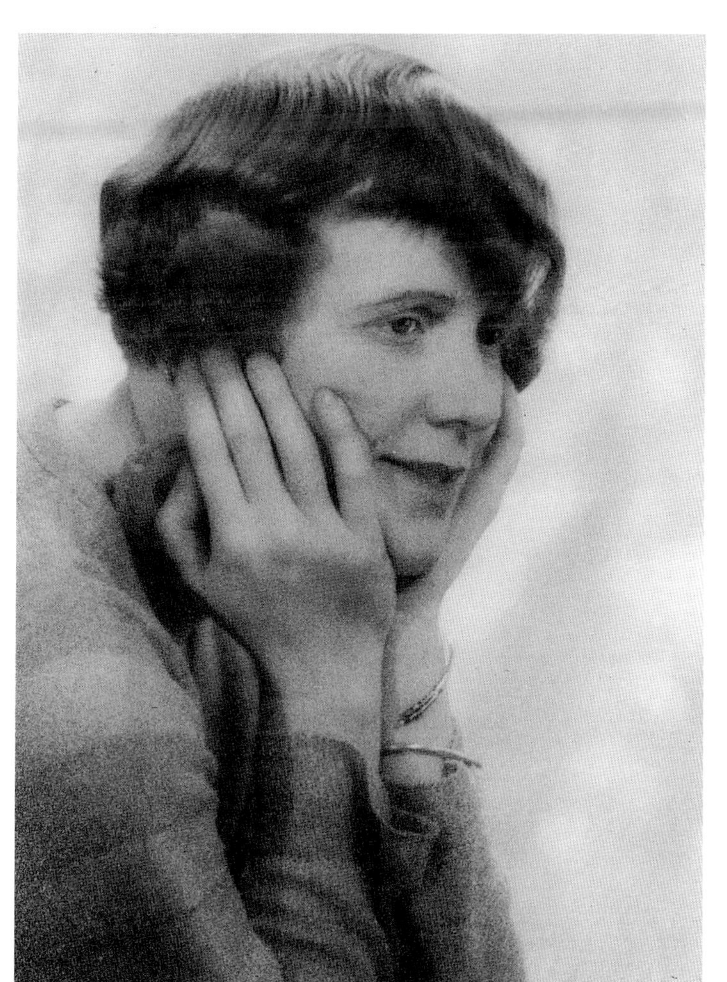

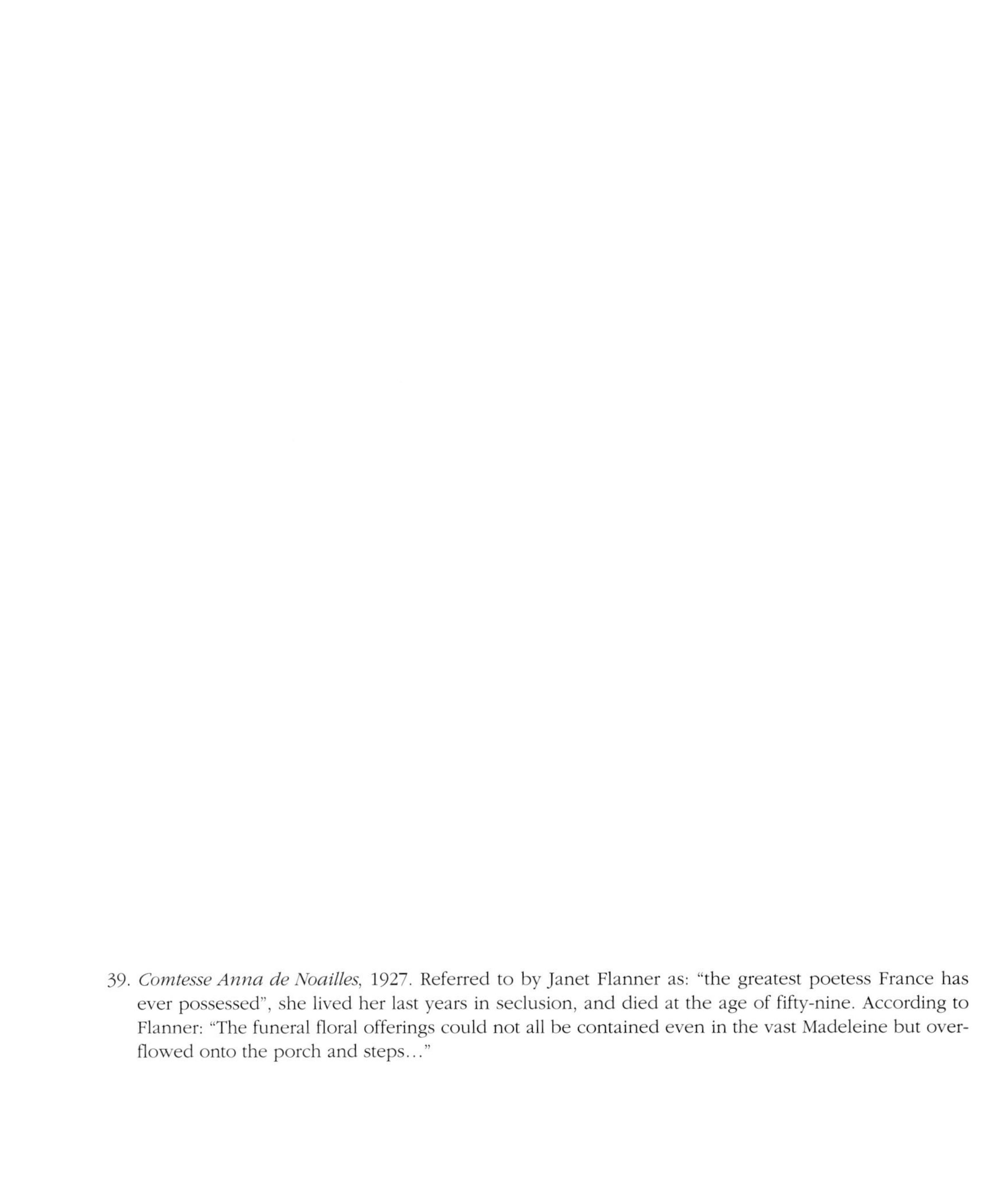

39. *Comtesse Anna de Noailles*, 1927. Referred to by Janet Flanner as: “the greatest poetess France has ever possessed”, she lived her last years in seclusion, and died at the age of fifty-nine. According to Flanner: “The funeral floral offerings could not all be contained even in the vast Madeleine but overflowed onto the porch and steps…”

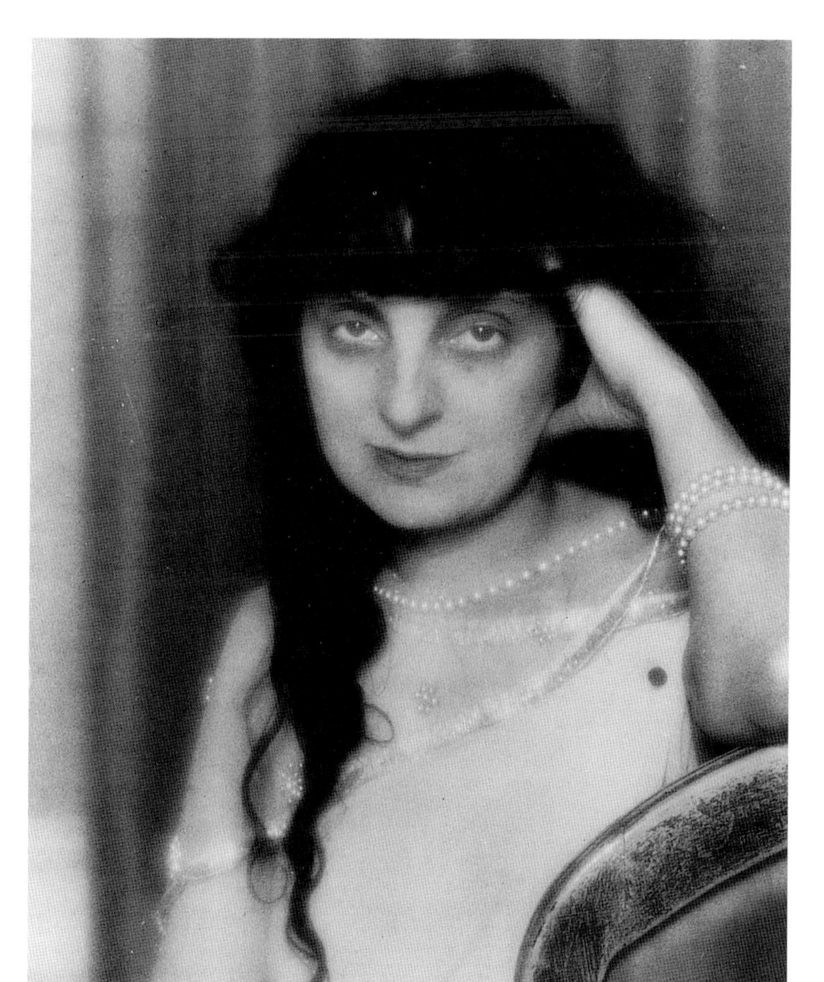

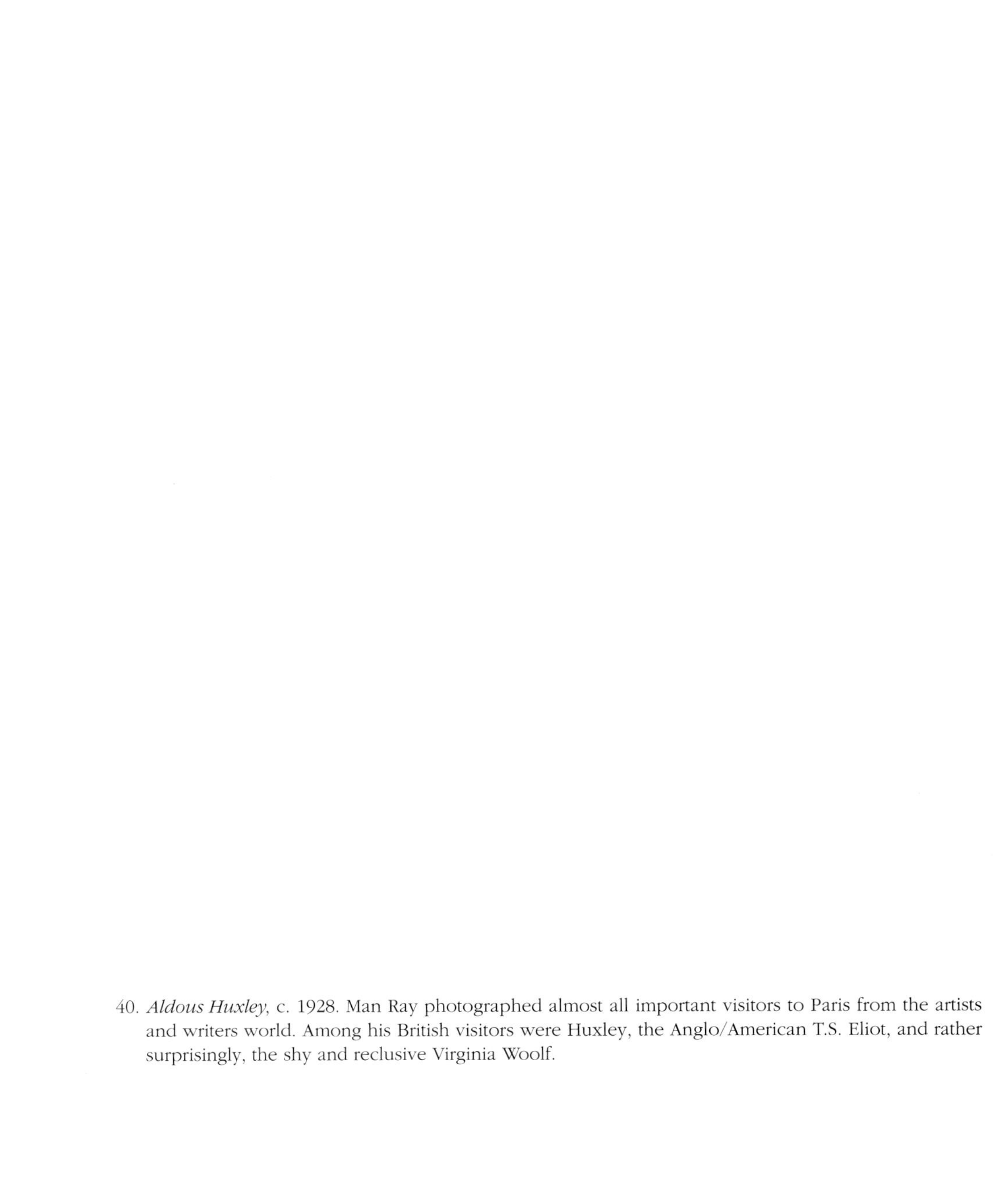

40. *Aldous Huxley*, c. 1928. Man Ray photographed almost all important visitors to Paris from the artists and writers world. Among his British visitors were Huxley, the Anglo/American T.S. Eliot, and rather surprisingly, the shy and reclusive Virginia Woolf.

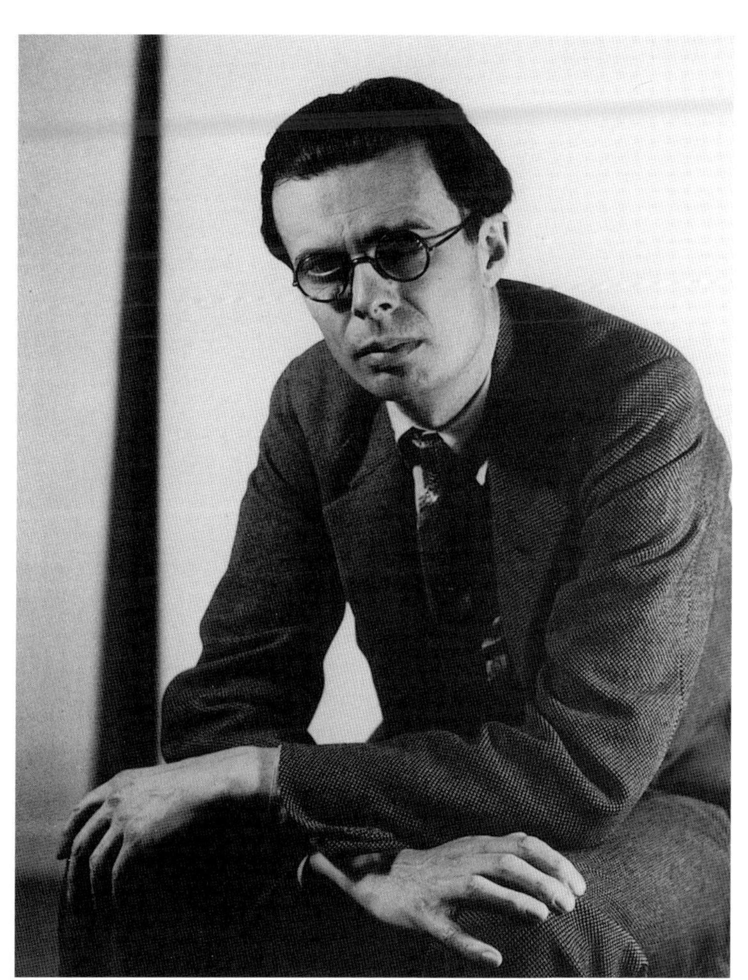

41. *Duchesse de Gramont*, late 1920s. A daughter of the ancient Ruspoli family of Rome, she became the third wife of the Duc de Gramont at the age of seventeen. Here, still appearing quite youthful and still in her thirties, she is already a widow.

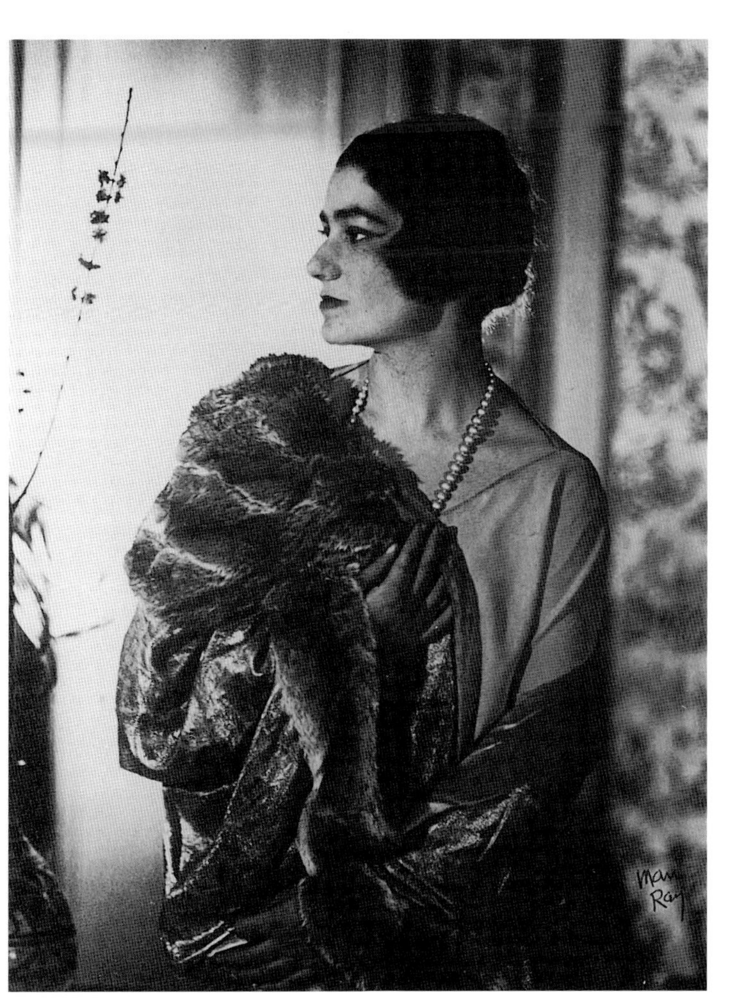

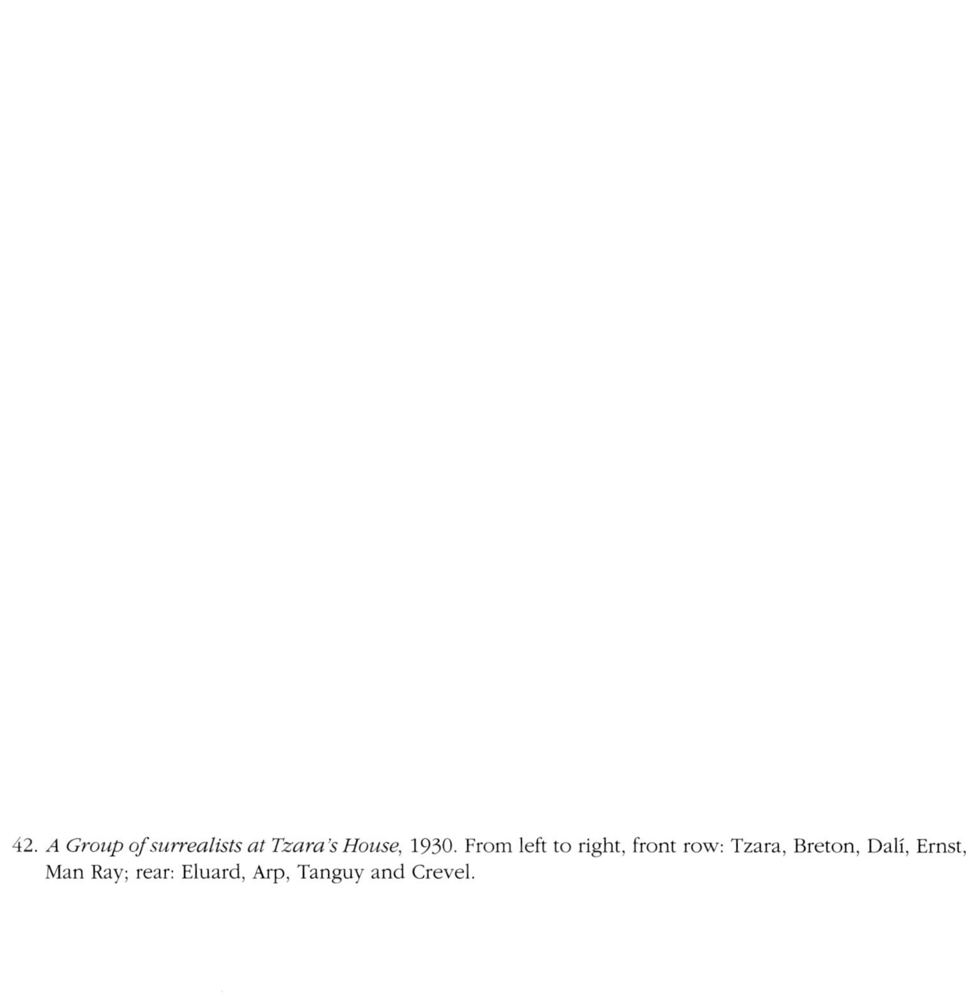

42. *A Group of surrealists at Tzara's House*, 1930. From left to right, front row: Tzara, Breton, Dalí, Ernst, Man Ray; rear: Eluard, Arp, Tanguy and Crevel.

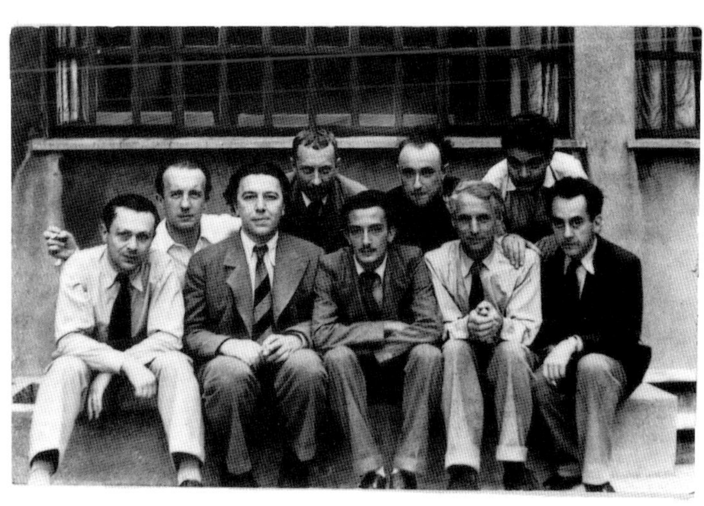

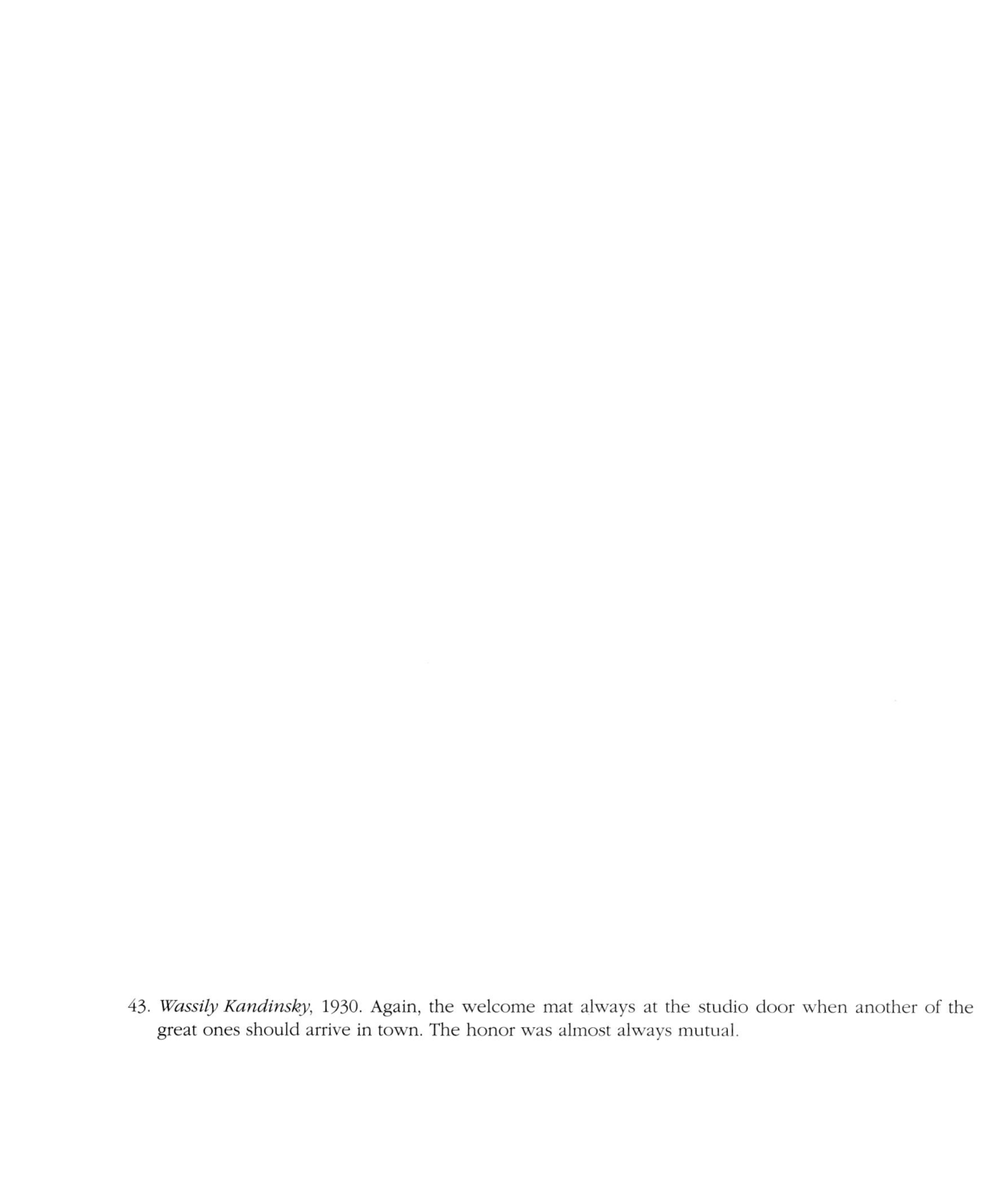

43. *Wassily Kandinsky*, 1930. Again, the welcome mat always at the studio door when another of the great ones should arrive in town. The honor was almost always mutual.

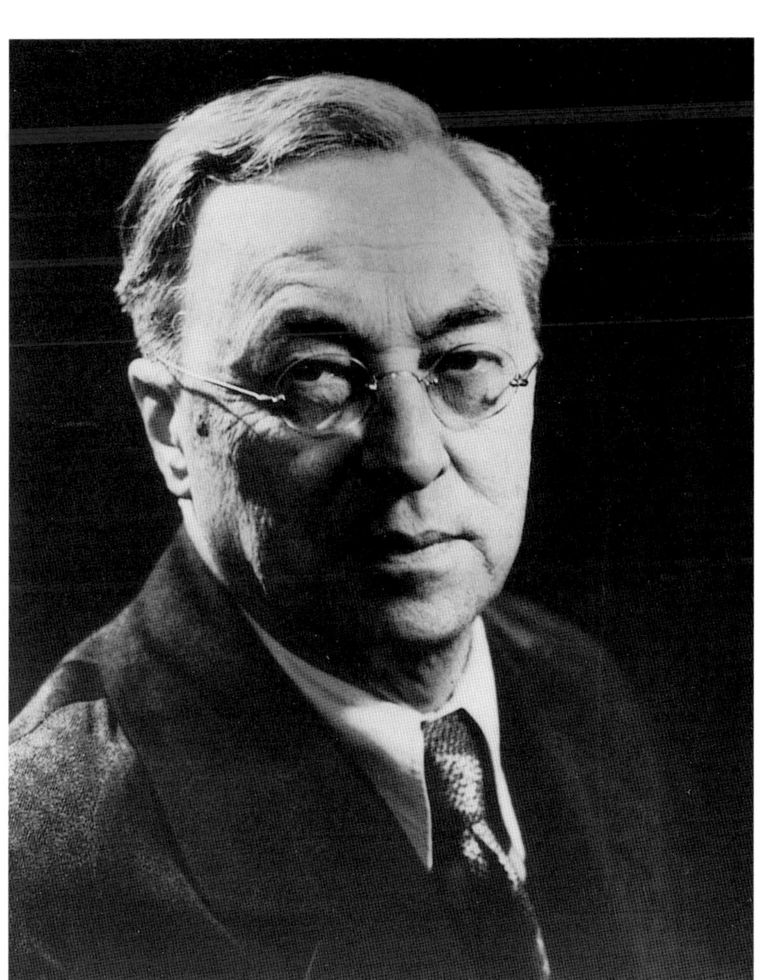

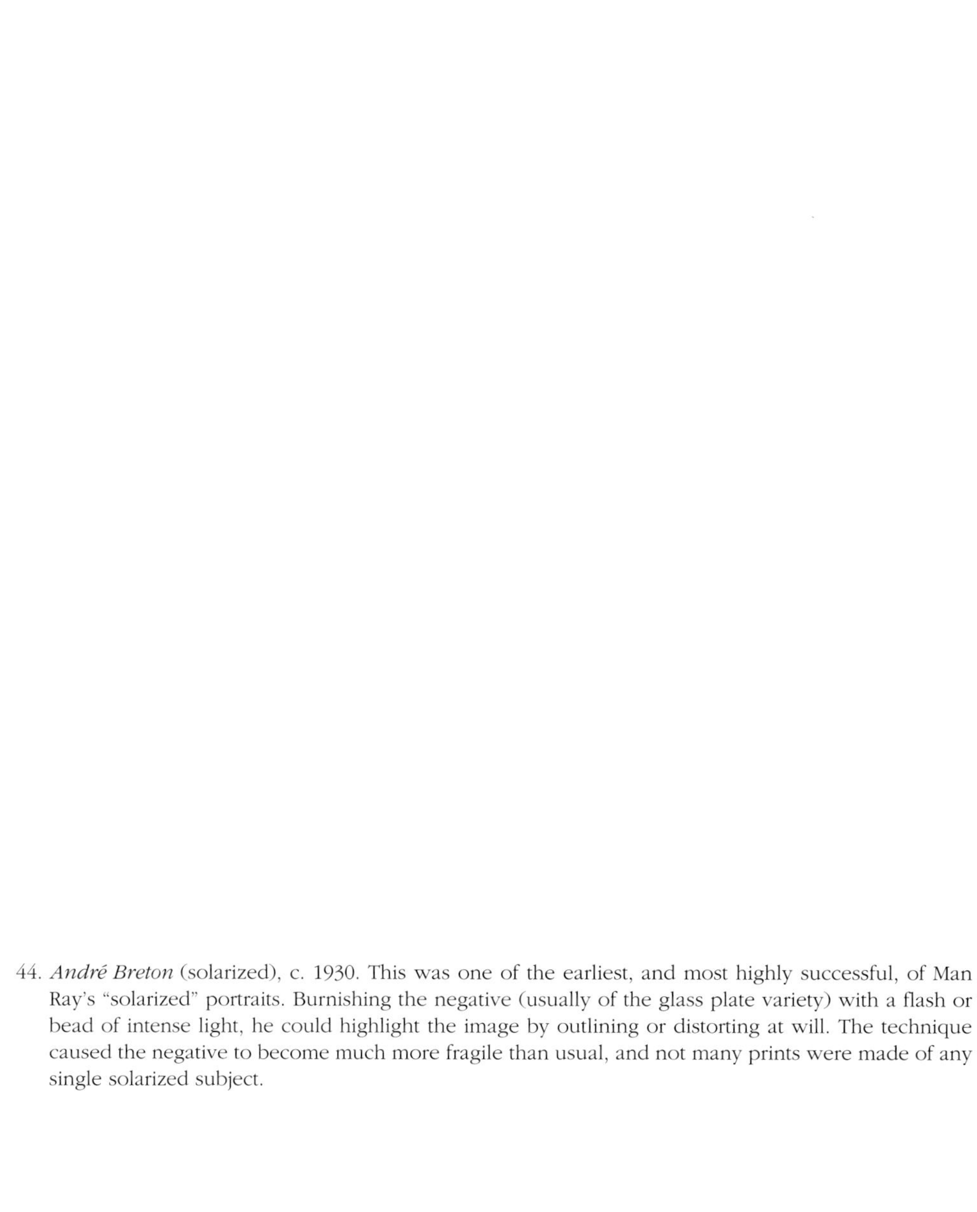

44. *André Breton* (solarized), c. 1930. This was one of the earliest, and most highly successful, of Man Ray's "solarized" portraits. Burnishing the negative (usually of the glass plate variety) with a flash or bead of intense light, he could highlight the image by outlining or distorting at will. The technique caused the negative to become much more fragile than usual, and not many prints were made of any single solarized subject.

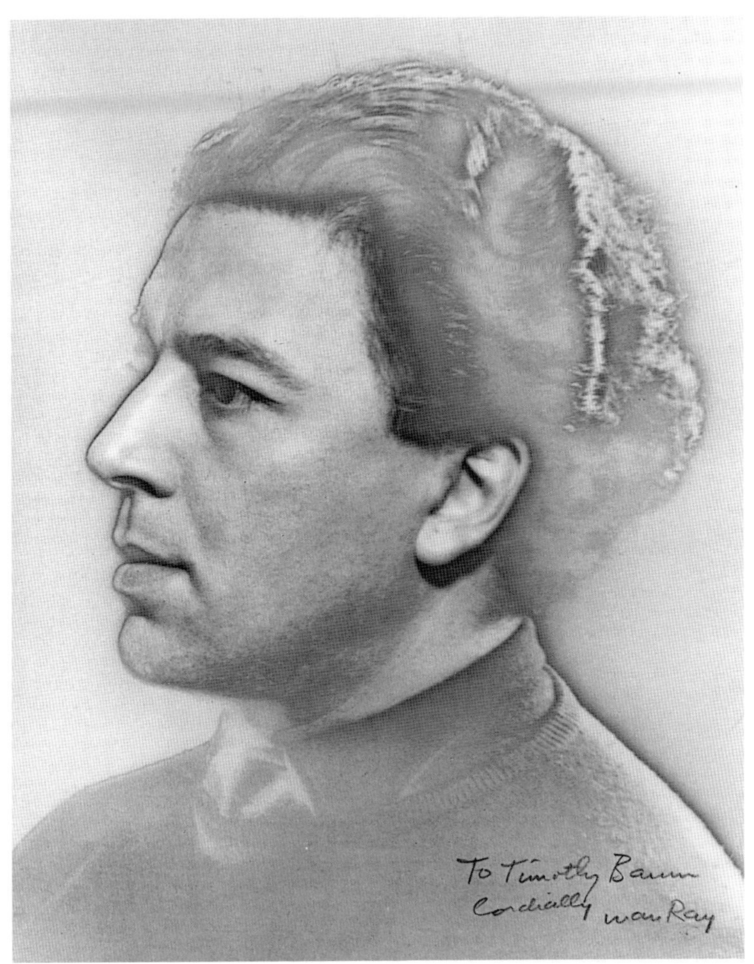
To Timothy Baum
Cordially Man Ray

45. *Marie-Berthe Aurenche*, 1930/1. Max Ernst's second (of four, and only French) wife, eventually abandoned by Ernst who turned his attention instead to the young English surrealist painter, Leonora Carrington.

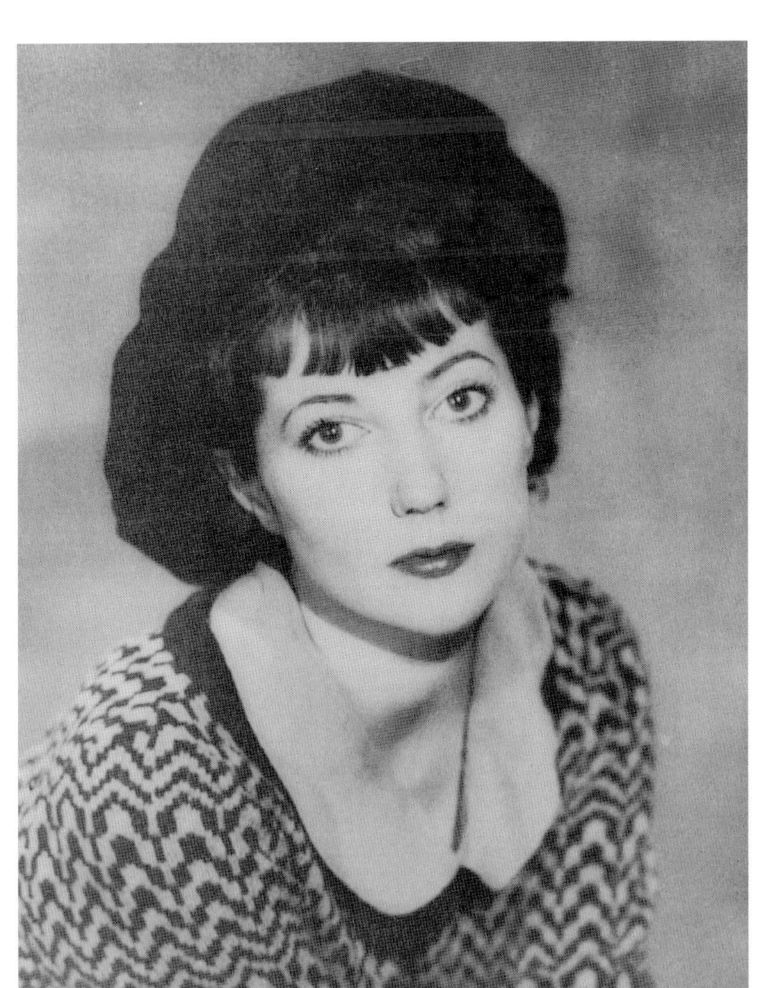

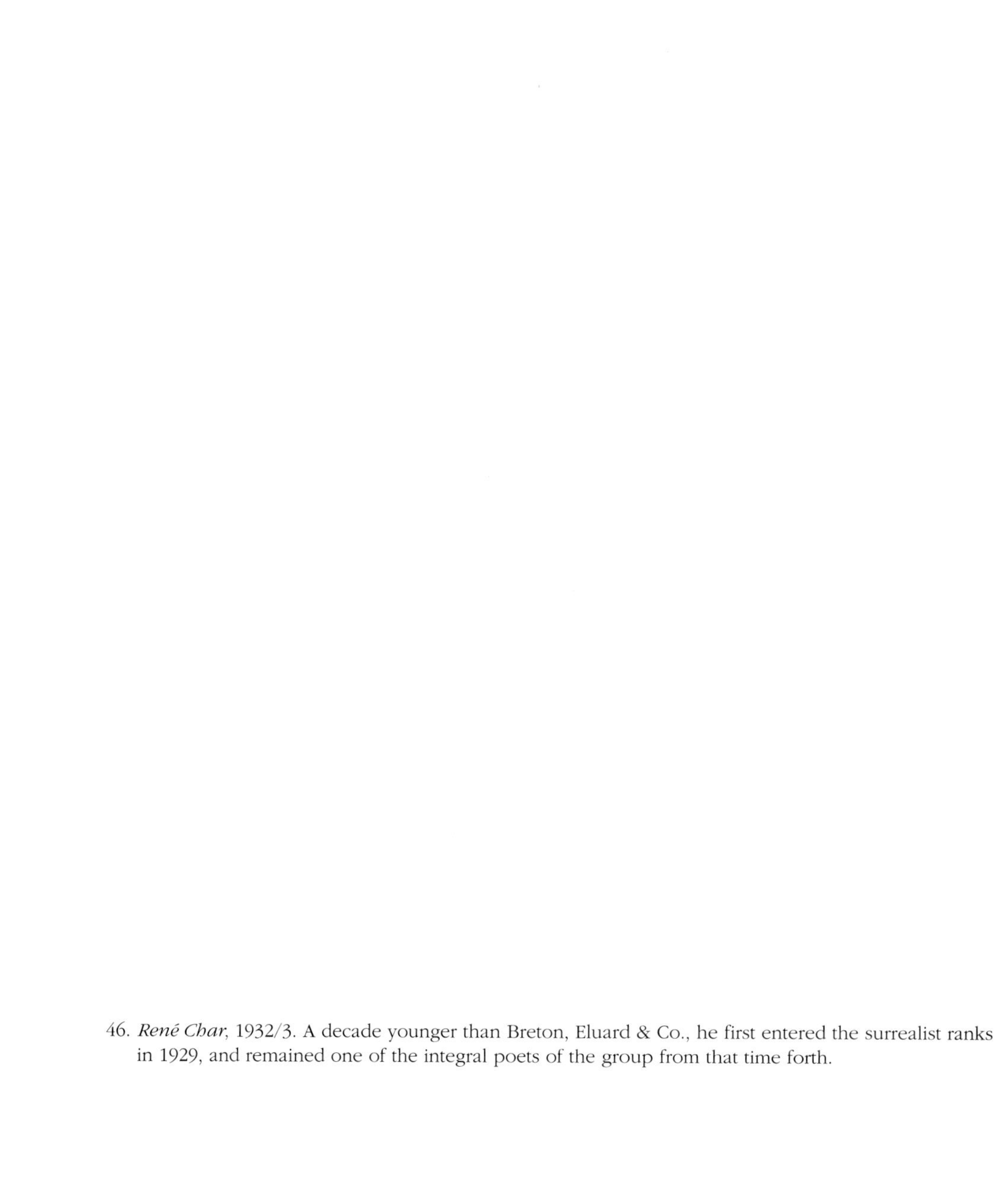

46. *René Char*, 1932/3. A decade younger than Breton, Eluard & Co., he first entered the surrealist ranks in 1929, and remained one of the integral poets of the group from that time forth.

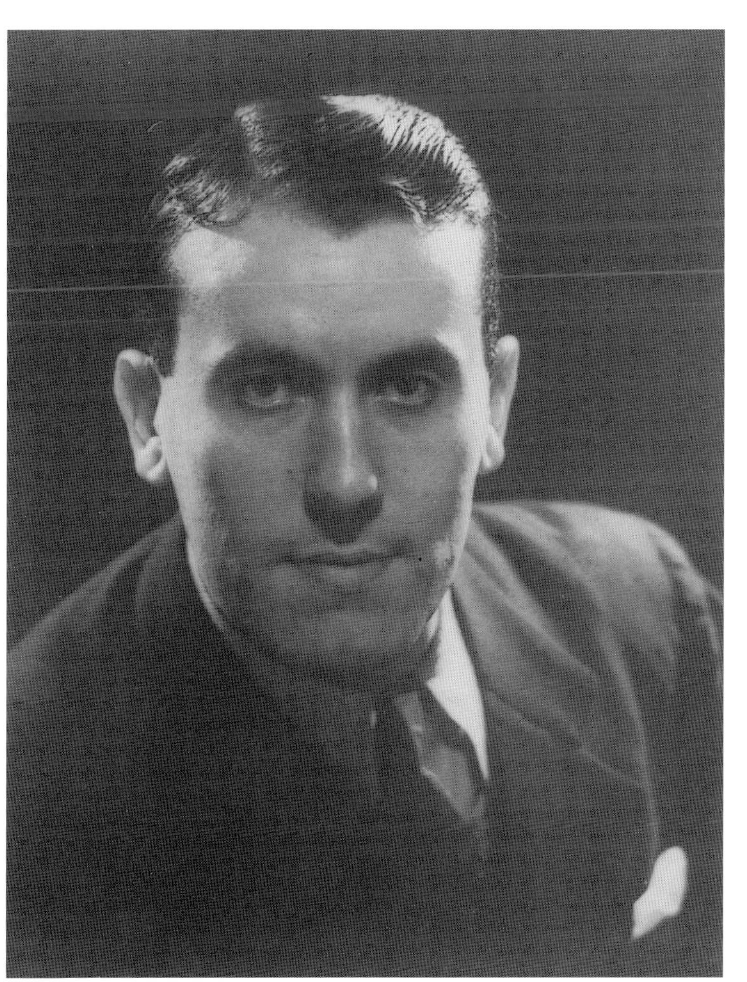

47. *Meret Oppenheim at the Printer's Wheel* (also known as *Erotique Voilée*), 1933. The pinnacle achievement of an interesting "shoot" at Marcoussis's etching atelier. Note that even though this particular print (one originating from Man Ray's own private collection) is dated 1935, it actually is an image from 1933 which subsequently appeared in *Minotaure* magazine, No. 5 (in May 1934).

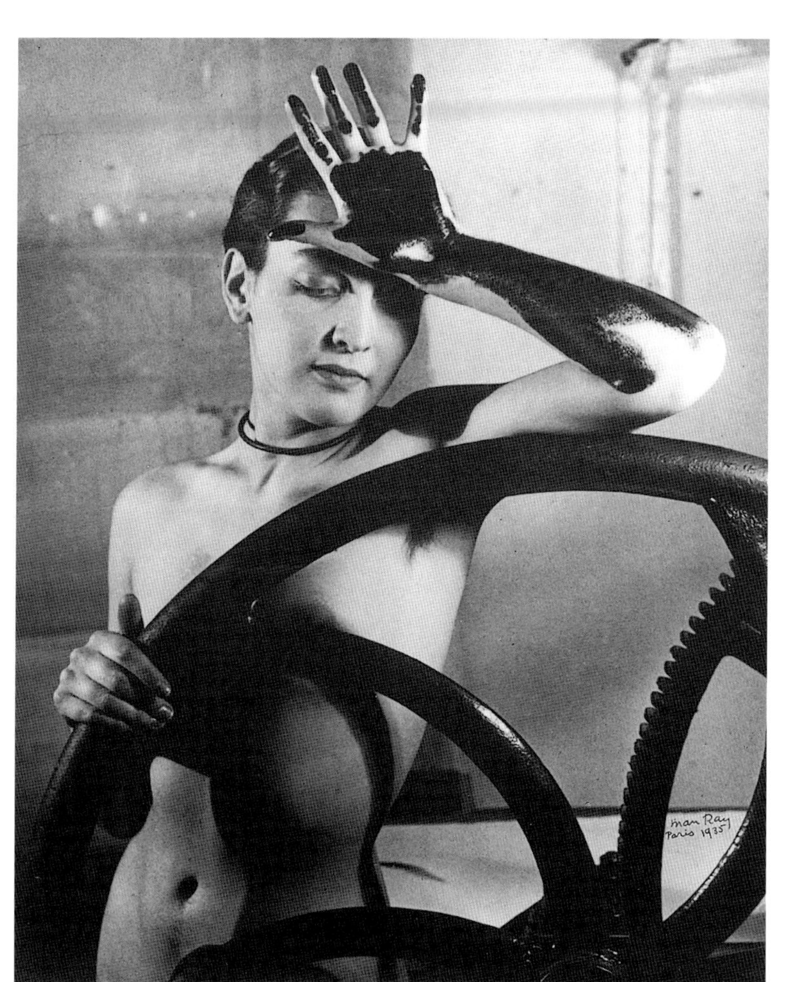
man Ray
Paris 1935

48. *Lady Diana Duff Cooper* (solarized), 1934. Another of Man Ray's elegant visitors from England. Originally Lady Diana Manners, daughter of the Duke of Rutland, she shocked her peers by attempting a career as an actress in films. She married Alfred Duff Cooper, who later became the British ambassador to France.

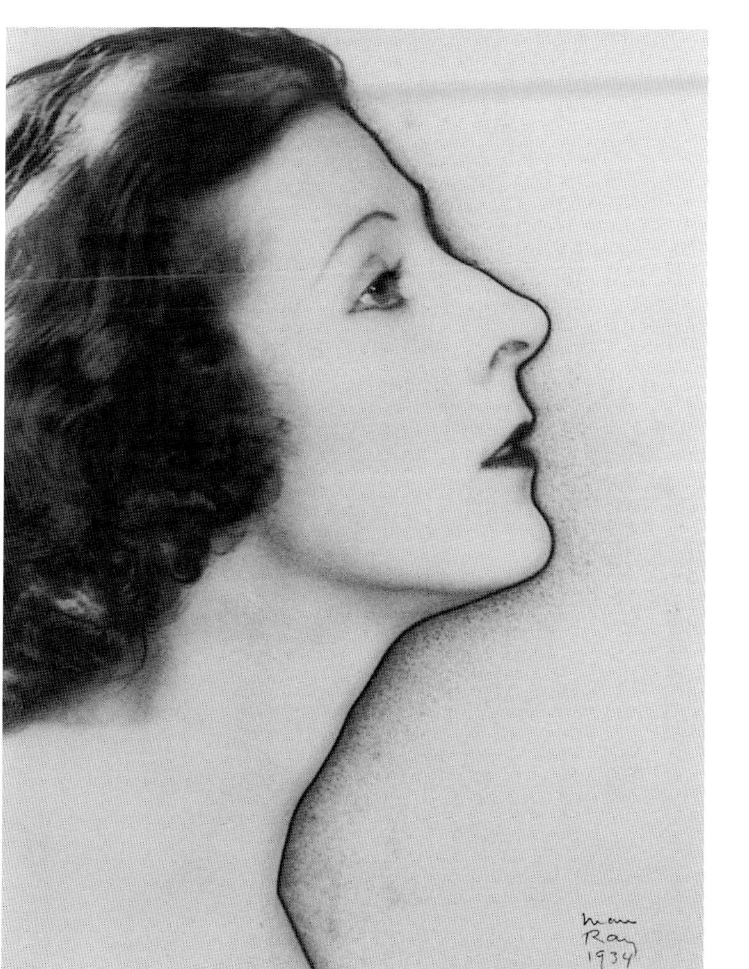
Man
Ray
1934

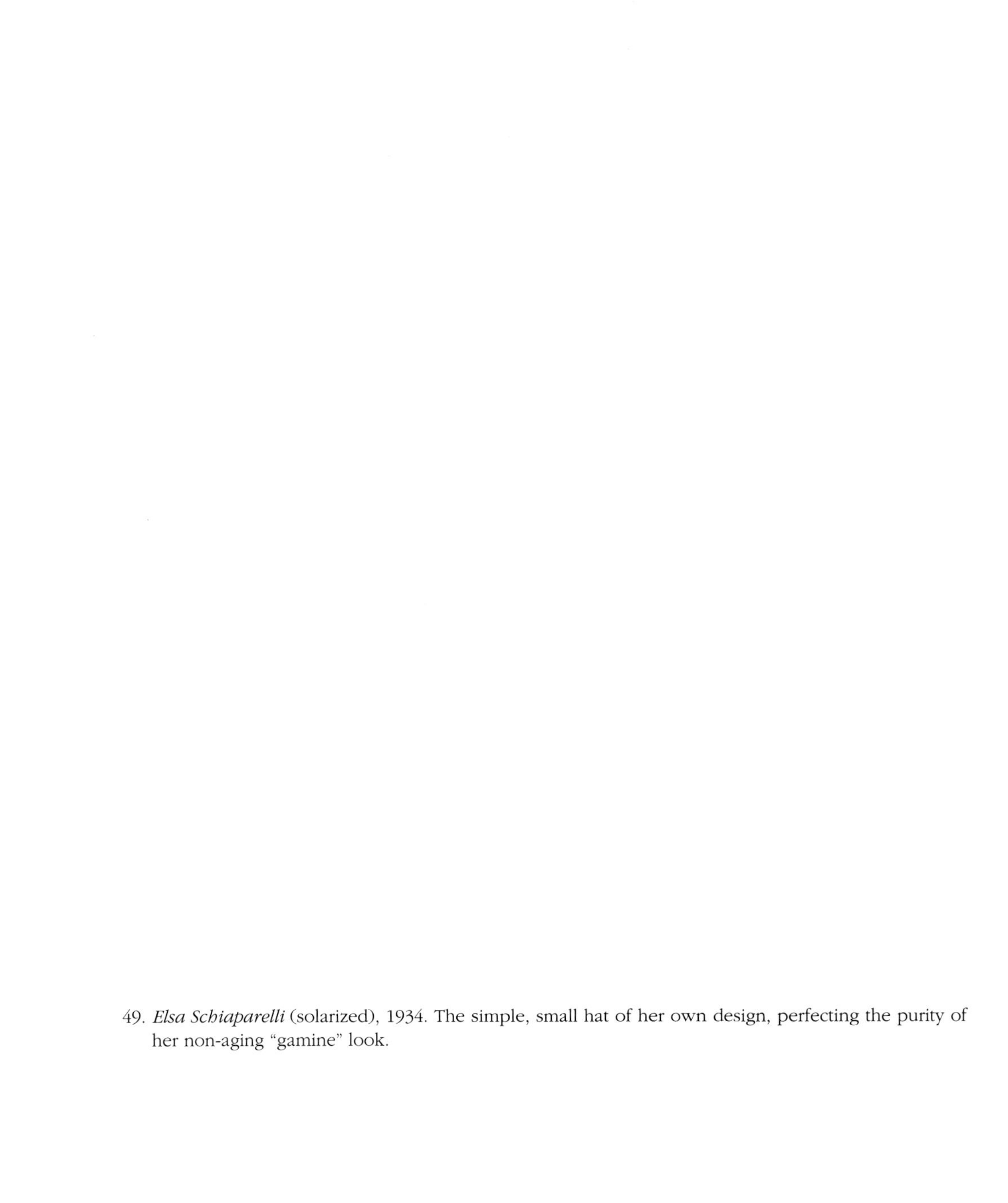

49. *Elsa Schiaparelli* (solarized), 1934. The simple, small hat of her own design, perfecting the purity of her non-aging "gamine" look.

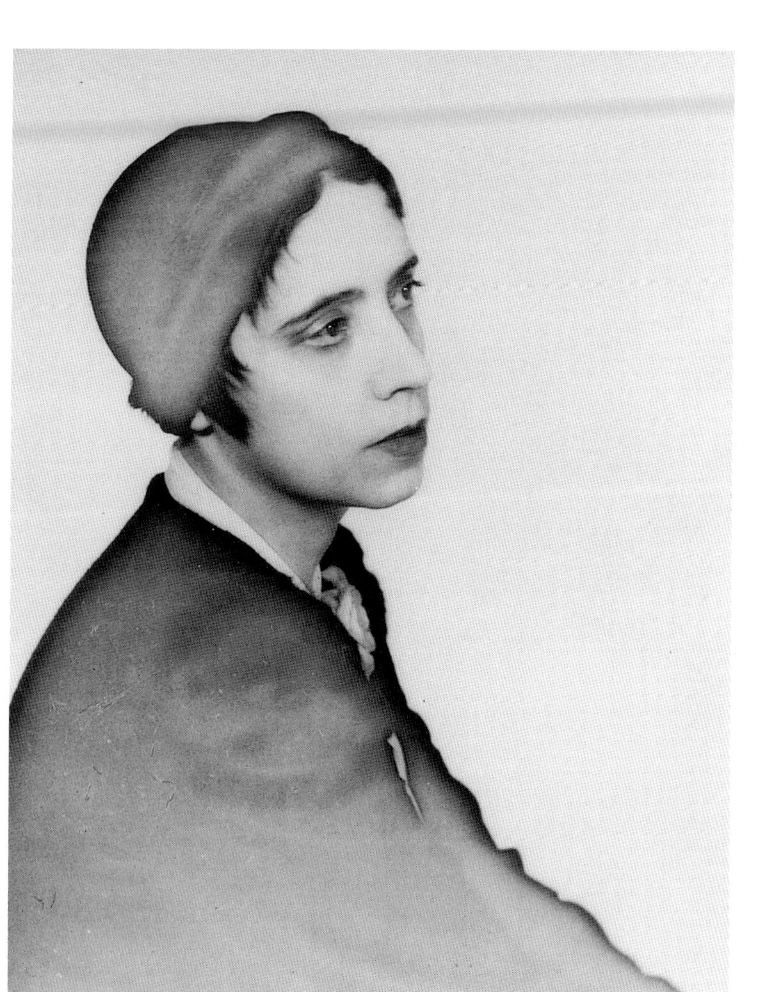

50. *Gisèle Prassinos Reading her Poems to Members of the surrealist Group*, 1934/5. The surrealists were always specialists in the art of "discovery". Here a solemn Breton and his twinklingly discerning cronies pay careful attention to their newest protegée, somewhere between her fourteenth and fifteenth birthdays, with her brother looking on in rapt admiration. From left to right: Jean-Marie Prassinos, André Breton, Henri Parisot, Paul Eluard (seated), Benjamin Peret, René Char and the young poetess herself.

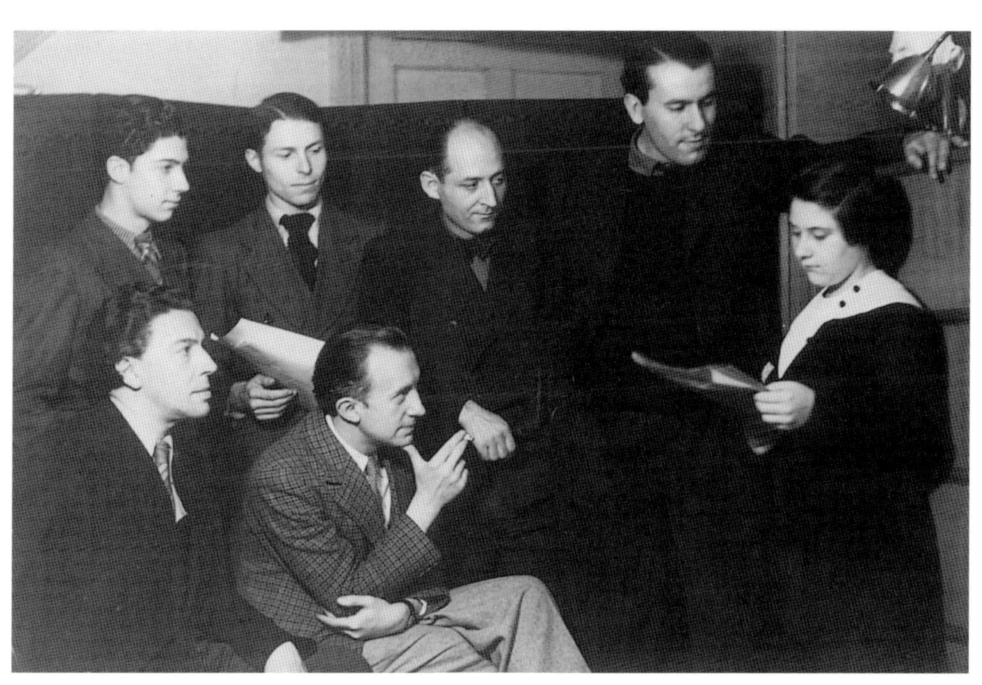

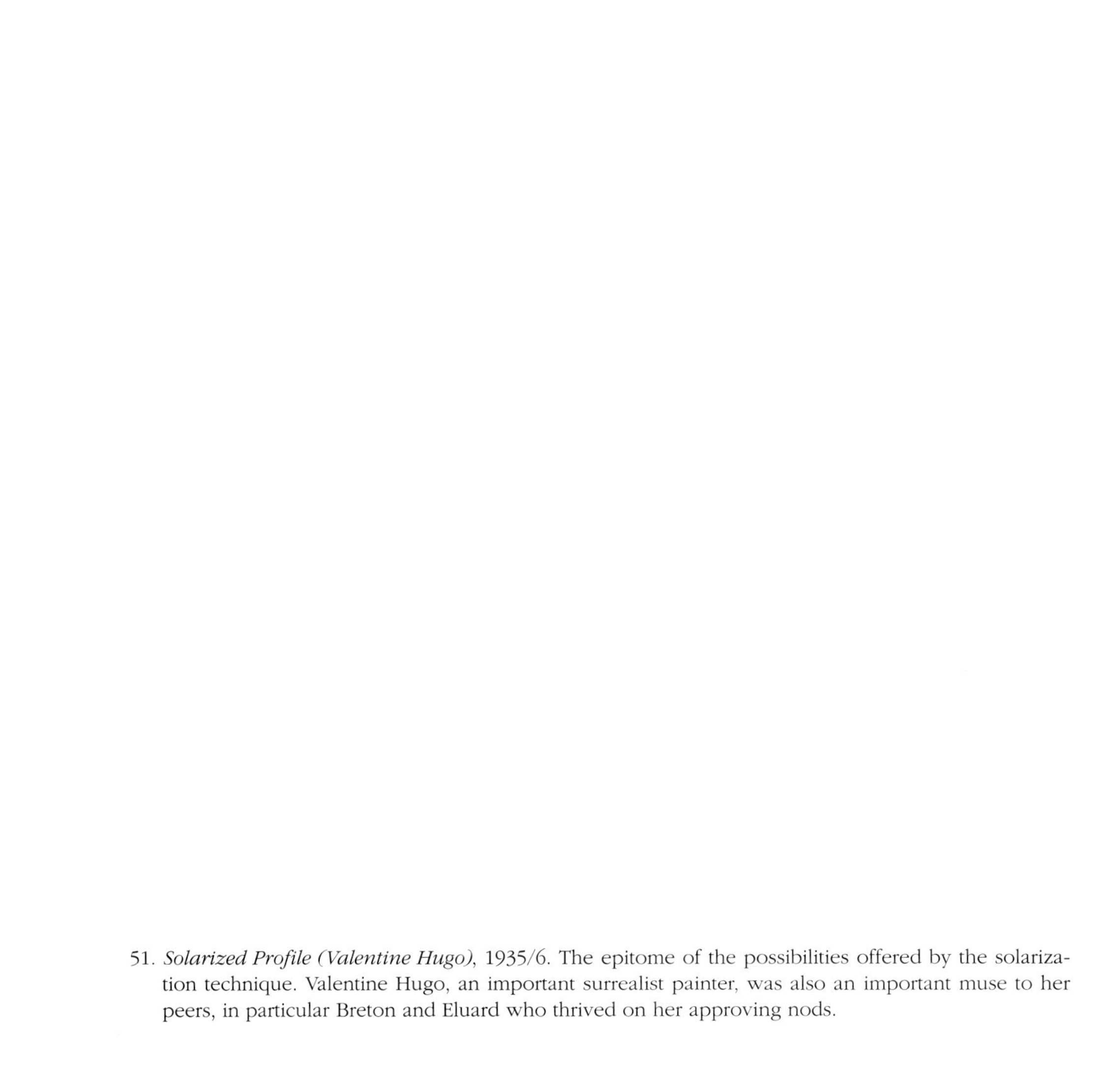

51. *Solarized Profile (Valentine Hugo)*, 1935/6. The epitome of the possibilities offered by the solarization technique. Valentine Hugo, an important surrealist painter, was also an important muse to her peers, in particular Breton and Eluard who thrived on her approving nods.

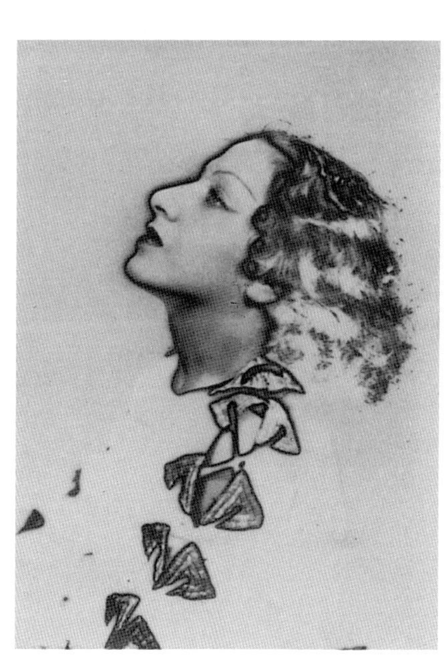

52. *Francis Picabia*, c. 1935. Multi-talented artist, poet and editor (his magazine, *391*, the ultimate publication of the Dada years). Perhaps the only artist (outdistancing even Picasso?) who journeyed through every major tendency in 20th Century painting, including Post-Impressionism and Post-War abstraction.

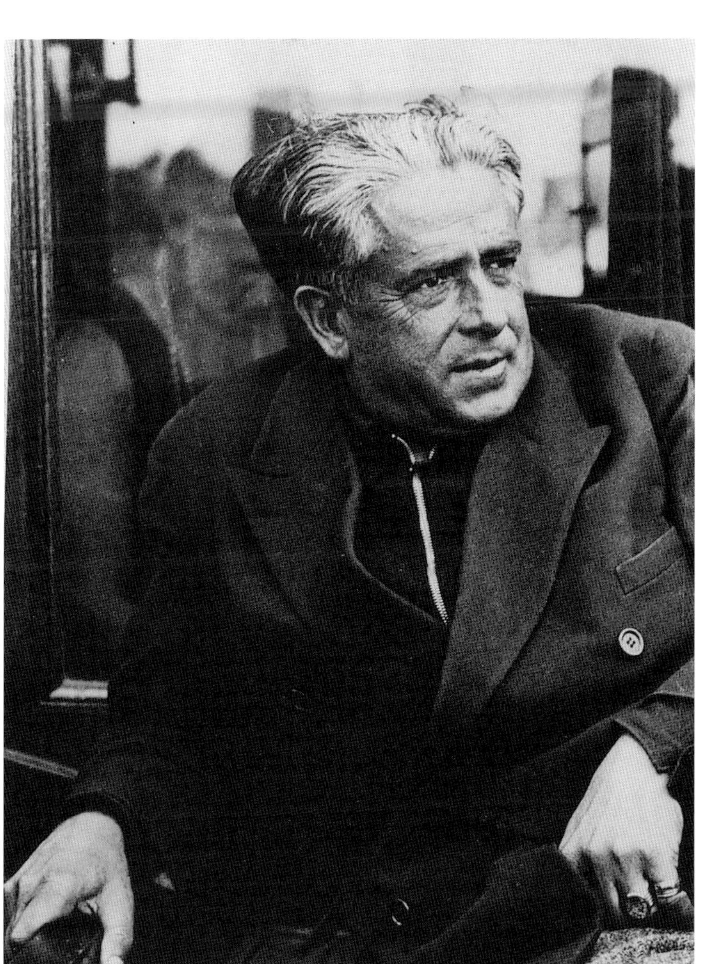

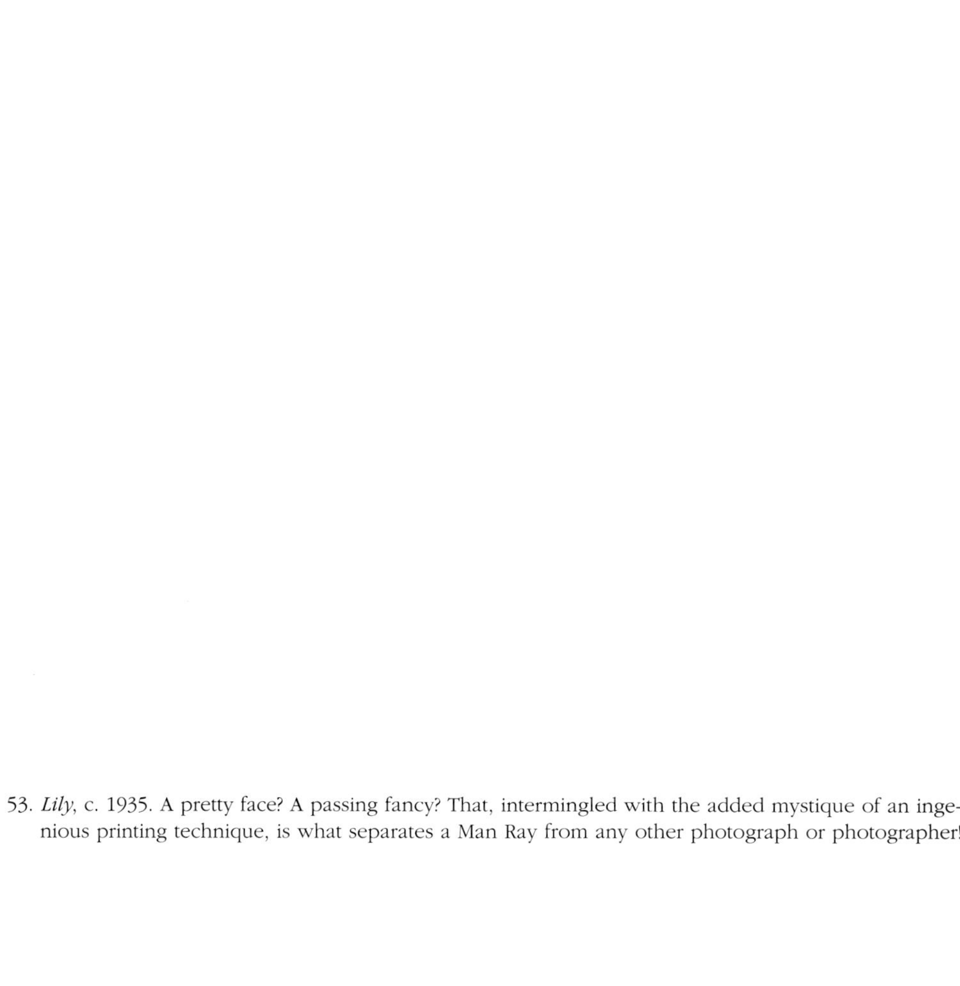

53. *Lily*, c. 1935. A pretty face? A passing fancy? That, intermingled with the added mystique of an ingenious printing technique, is what separates a Man Ray from any other photograph or photographer!

54. *Léon Blum*, 1935/6. Leader of the French Socialist Party; devoted personal friend and admirer of Man Ray.

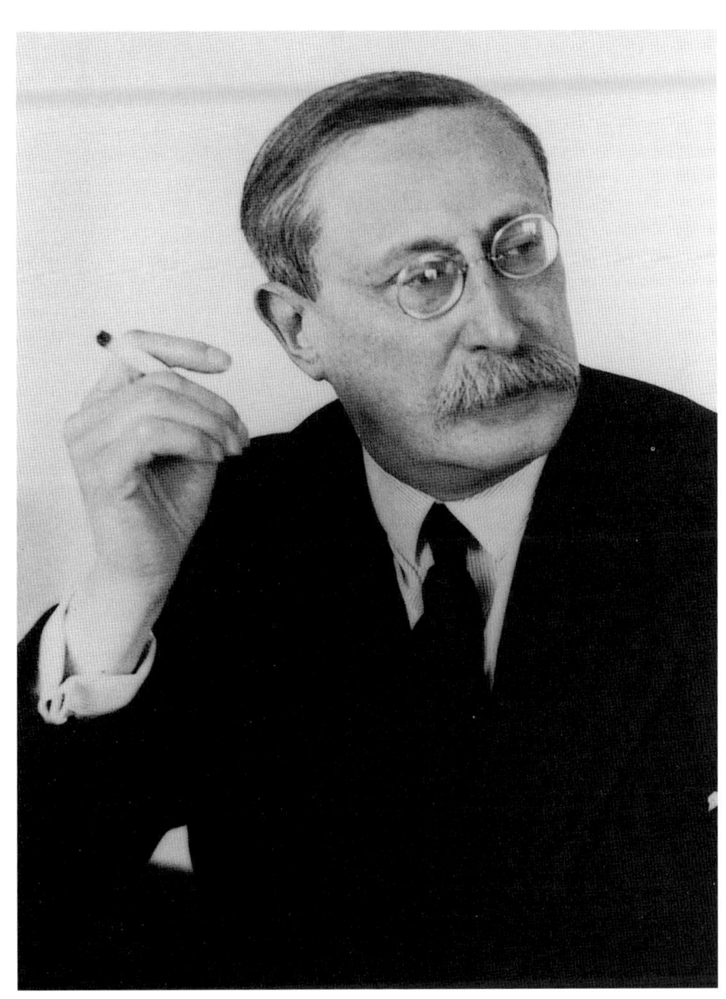

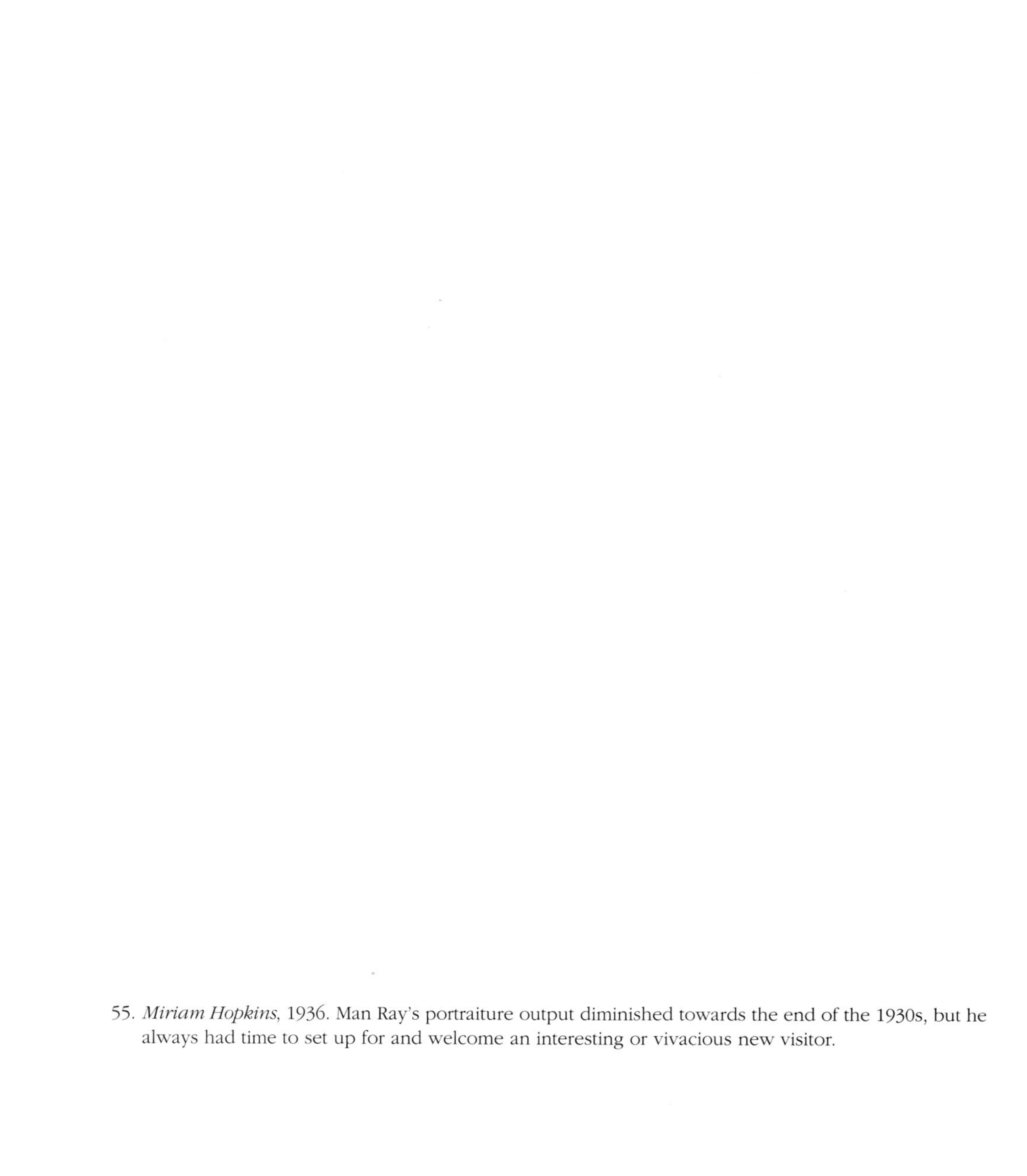

55. *Miriam Hopkins*, 1936. Man Ray's portraiture output diminished towards the end of the 1930s, but he always had time to set up for and welcome an interesting or vivacious new visitor.

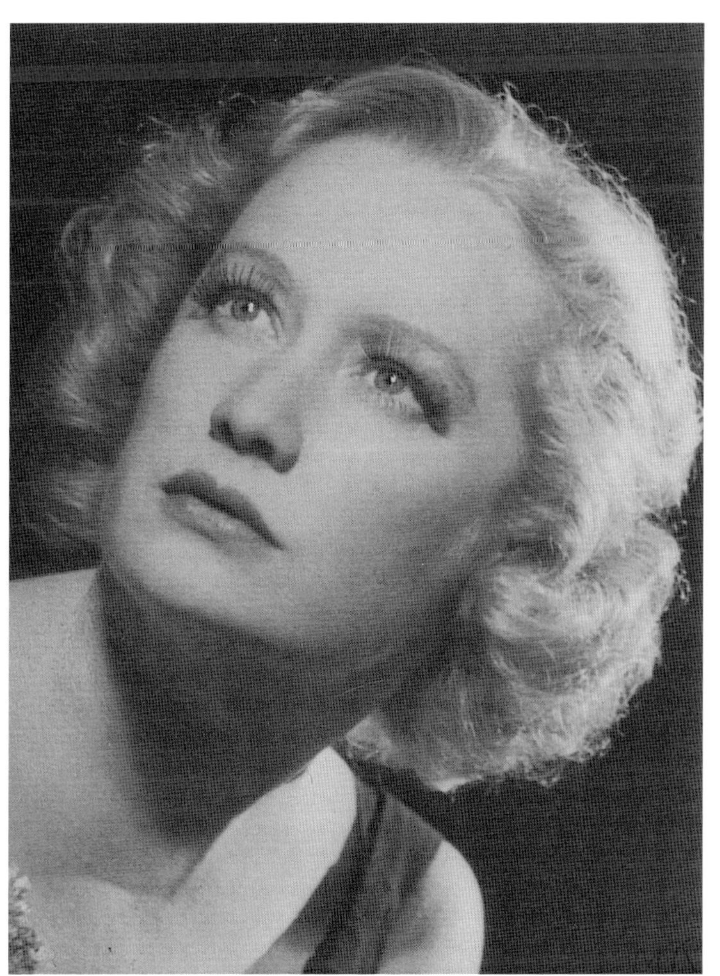

56. *Paul Eluard in Uniform*, 1939. The full circle. Called up at the end of 1914, after almost two years in a Swiss sanatorium recovering from tuberculosis, Eluard served at the front, then was hospitalized after being gassed. During a leave in 1917 he married an unforgettable young Russian, Hélène Dimitrovnia Diakanova, who he had met in the Davos sanatorium and upon whom he had bestowed the nickname "Gala". The marriage survived until 1930 when Gala succumbed to the bewitchment cast by a persistent and charming young Spaniard who had entered her life, and finally enjoined with the Spaniard, Señor Salvador Dalí. Eluard grew to become the other most illustrious poet of the Dada/surrealist era, alongside Breton. In 1939, with the threat of war become a reality, Eluard was mobilized a second time, and rejoined his regiment. The following year, Man Ray, as so many others, departed his beloved Paris as well: "With a farewell look at my studio and the feeling that I would never see it again, that twenty years of work was being wiped out, I locked the door."

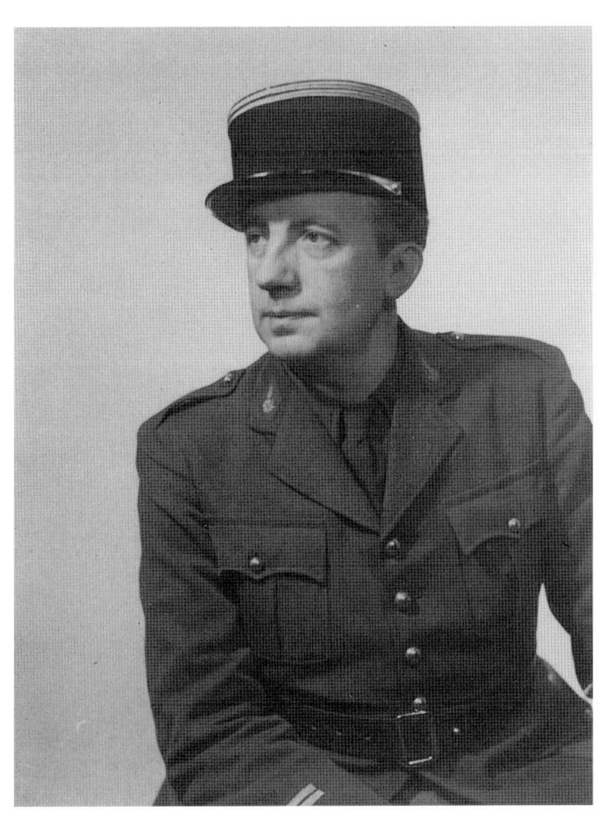

List of Plates